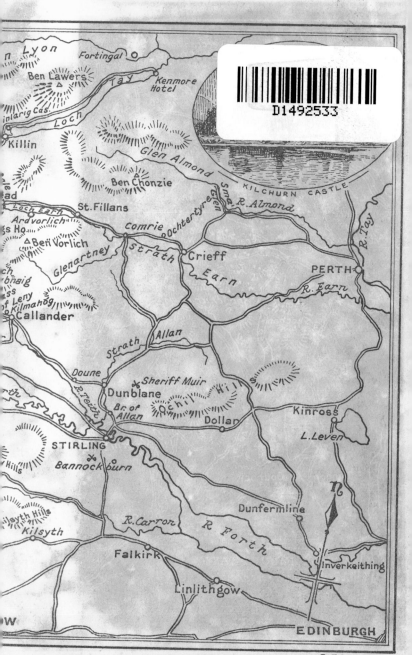

n Lyon
Fortingal
Ben Lawers
Kenmore
Hotel
Tay
inlarig Cas.
Loch
Killin
Glen Almond
KILCHURN CASTLE
Ben Chonzie
ad
Loch Earn
St. Fillans
R. Almond
Ardvorlich
Comrie
Ochtertyre
R. Tay
ss Hq
Ben Vorlich
Strath
Crieff
ch
Glenartney
Earn
PERTH
bnaig
ss
R. Earn
of Leny
Kilmahog
Callander
Strath
Allan
Doune
Sheriff Muir
rth
Dunblane
Ochil Hills
R. Teith
Br of
Allan
Dollar
Kinross
L. Leven
STIRLING
Bannock burn
Hills
n
Dunfermline
lsyth Hills
R. Carron
R Forth
Kilsyth
Falkirk
Inverkeithing
Linlithgow
ow
EDINBURGH

E. F. Inkster

HIGHLANDS, HIGHWAYS
AND HEROES

IN GLENLYON

Highlands, Highways and Heroes

or Wanderings in the Westlands

BY

D. C. CUTHBERTSON, F.R.G.S.

WITH 31 ILLUSTRATIONS

EDINBURGH

ROBERT GRANT & SON

126 PRINCES STREET

1931

TO
LINDSAY

Printed in Great Britain
by Turnbull & Spears, Edinburgh

PREFACE

THIS book grew from the chance question of a boy.
It was my pleasant duty to impart to him all that
I knew—and it is little enough, unfortunately—
about our native wild flowers. It was a rare week-
end that our vasculum was not heavy with trophies,
and many happy hours we spent in examining,
classifying and drying our treasures.

One day we went in search of a certain plant
which is to be found in damp, mossy land, and our
quest took us by Loch Sloy. While resting on a
bank, to pass the idle hour I recounted one or two
of the traditions connected with the glen. From
that day ere we adventured to a new hunting-
ground, in self-defence I had perforce to make
myself familiar with the feuds and folklore of the
district, until the glamour of the thing so enfolded
me that I became an enthusiast and spared neither
time nor trouble to find out all that I could about
this wonderful Westland which lies at our door.

Much that I have been told by natives was
so obviously unreliable that I have omitted many
things. Not a little that I have gleaned from
books ancient and modern to my great regret I

5

cannot acknowledge, because I have forgotten or mislaid my authorities.

Gladly do I pay homage to Chambers's "Book of Days" and the same author's "Picture of Scotland"; to Gilpin's "Highlands in Scotland" and Pennant's "Tour in Scotland"; Marshall's "Perthshire," Nimmo's "Stirlingshire," and Robertson's "Ayrshire"; Cheviot's "Proverbs"; "History of the Clan Macfarlane"; and not least to Sir Walter Scott from many sources. The evenings spent by quiet lochs and hill-sides, conning these books and endeavouring mentally to stage the scenes as the sun was going down behind the rampart of bens; changing the prospect from gold to purple, in turn to crimson and blood red, fading to shadow; and the great stillness which envelops the lonely glens, when our wood fire became even as a companion, are amongst the happiest hours of my life.

So too would I express my thanks to the editors of the *Sheffield Independent*, *Birmingham Gazette*, *Yorkshire Observer*, and *Northern Echo*, for permission to reproduce such articles as first saw the light in their columns. To the *Daily Express* for their enthusiastic welcome to some of these chapters which really gave the book its title. To the late St John Adcock and the editor of *Public Opinion* for help and kindly advice. To David Anderson of the L.M.S. Railway; Bryce B.

Morrison of the *Glasgow Herald* and my brother for invaluable photographic aid, and to my friend Sydney Chamberlin for the care and trouble he has taken with the reproductions.

I claim nothing for this book, and if my readers find errors or wrong deductions, remember it is not a history and possesses no intention other than of being a record of a season which was for me a radiantly happy one, rich in memories which can never again recur.

D. C. C.

April 1931

CONTENTS

LIST OF ILLUSTRATIONS

Highlands, Highways
and Heroes

I

FROM MY WINDOW

Call of the blood in the open road,
  Whispering winds from the sea.
Call of the glens and the lonely bens—
  You call to the heart of me !

THE open road calls to most hearts when the spring
sun mounts high. Whether we are gangrels at the
core for all our black coats and business affairs, I
cannot say, but there is a something deep-rooted
within us which sends the blood coursing again when
we hear a mavis in the garden or read a tale of the
hills.

This morning I suddenly realised that winter was
now over, and if the snow still caps the bens, or lies
here and there like a white patch on a dark hill-side,
the roads are open and the burns are singing a free
song again.

The frost is sweirt to go and still powders the
morning grass, but the sun is growing stronger and
braver, and a strange unrest is apparent amongst
the birds. Very soon, at this rate, the foolish
March hare will commence his amorous gambols
on the brae-side and the lark will trill again against
a blue sky.

My old tortoise is out and about, and I saw him amongst the dead leaves at the garden-foot this morning, as if even his sluggish blood feels the urge to be up and out of doors.

The thrushes have taken the grassy patch into their control, and brave fellows they look in their brown-and-white waistcoats; while in the old elms that back the garden—grey old veterans which have seen many seasons come and go — the rooks are making quite a fuss over some domestic affairs, and there seems no end to their squabbles.

To me it is the sweet o' the year, and I share the universal unrest—the urge to go afield amongst the glens or hedgerows.

The dark days are past ; a cosy fire and the drawn curtain have lost charm when everywhere brown is giving place to green and sap is bringing new life to the moribund woods. The snell east wind has enjoyed its season, and now—

> It's a warm wind, the west wind,
> Full of birds' cries.

From my window as I sit I can see the hills. Not the stern, rugged bens, purple clad, but hills green even in the distance, where white moving specks which I know are sheep crop all the day long in the home of the whaup and the peesweep.

To-day they are quiet and lonely enough; peaceful too in the spring sunlight, and behind them reaches a blue haze of distance.

On one hill-side is a white farm-house, and in the autumn it grows in size as a landmark as the stack-yard gradually fills ; but now the fodder is con-

COVENANTER COMMUNION CUP

LUSS VILLAGE AND BEN LOMOND

sumed and it seems shrunken and derelict. Too far off to observe smoke from its chimneys, as the gloaming creeps over the country-side and a light suddenly springs up in a window, I know the long day is over, the kye are bedded down for the night, and the rest hour has come.

Perhaps it acts as a beacon to some late traveller on the moorland road, and it looks bright and homely, poor lamp as it must be, but long before my bedtime arrives it suddenly disappears, the last sign of life away there on the hill, and another clean, healthy day has come and gone.

I know, although it is far off from where I sit, how utterly silent it is away there on the brae-side. Still to eeriness, but for the occasional querulous cry of the peesweep, suspicious alike of friend and foe and restless as the sea.

Some say the peesweep has a guilty conscience and cannot rest like other flesh and blood. There is one eerie story about it having mocked the Saviour on the Cross, but that apart, its misdeeds of later years are enough to haunt it for generations yet to come, and some country folks look upon it as accursed.

The lore and legend of the past is gradually dying out, but the score against this beautiful bird—and it is one of the most beautiful, I think—is too full to be easily forgotten or forgiven.

The hills I see through the glasses from my window were Covenanting country in the bad old days. Many a poor, starving, outlawed creature sought refuge amongst their hollows, hunted through moor and moss-hag, clinging to life when

all but life was taken from them, and then the peesweep would whirl and wheel and cry about their
hidieholes, so that the dragoons might hunt them
down.

No wonder the simple country people of those
days looked upon the bird as an enemy spy, an
emissary of the evil one, and still believe that its ill
conscience deprives it of peace and rest.

Over there, hidden from my view to-day, was the
home of Pollok, author of " The Course of Time,"
a man whose work is being forgotten but can never
die.

He entered into Nature's holy place,
Her inner Chamber, and beheld her face.

Amongst the moorlands lies Lochgoin, the home
of John Howie, with its relics and mementoes of the
" Killing times."   Not far away is the little village
of Fenwick, where it is said the dragoons played at
football in the street with a martyr's head.   It may
be so, I cannot tell, so many are the tales, so lichen-
grown by time that one must accept these traditions
on faith, or agree to forget or ignore.

An old kirk-yard epitaph records the incident :

Here lieth one whom bloody Inglis shot,
By birth a monster rather than a Scot,
Who that his monstrous extract might be seen,
Cut off his head, then kicked it o'er the green ;
This was the head that was to wear a crown,
A foot-ball made by a profane dragoon.

They had a dreadful time these same Covenanters,
and some of the privations they voluntarily endured
form a remarkable epoch in Scottish Church history.

Strange turn of the wheel that John Knox and Bloody Claverhouse should both take their brides from under the same Ayrshire roof!

One of my cherished possessions is a Communion Cup used at open-air Conventicles. Formed not unlike a modern egg-cup, the stem unscrews and it all fits into one piece again so as to be easily concealed or carried on the person.

The intimidating " Highland Host " which swept Ayrshire and Galloway districts would doubtless return to their native glens by the Fenwick moor roads. Loaded with booty and the pillaged treasures of many a farm and cottage, they thought it no crime to oppress the Whigs.

" Bloody Clavers," who was looked upon in the western Lowlands as a demon incarnate, a man whose very soul was stained with innocent blood, whose fiendish cruelty nothing could appease, was viewed from a totally different angle by the Highlanders. To them he was " Ian mor nan Cath," or " Great John of the Battles," a mighty leader and a loyal champion of the King.

Indomitable, fighting men all ; who would change a page of the sometimes harrowing history of the West, for it formed character, bred a hardy independence which has stood their descendants in good stead on many occasions and throughout the world?

The feuds in Ayrshire and Renfrewshire were as bitter and ruthless as any amongst the hot-blooded Highland clans, and the King's writ was of no more account in Carrick and Cunningham than in the outermost isles.

To us to-day, living in an environment where the

B

law is all-powerful and no man can carry on a blood feud with his neighbour, these bad old days seem almost incredible—or at least to belong to romance. But not so—and this tale of bloodshed engendered by a sheep's head is a rather grim jest !

The scene was on Lugarside, that Ayrshire stream made classic through the fastidious taste of a Burns' contemporary, because in the beautiful song associated with this river the original water was the Stinchar, but as it did not sound euphonious enough for the poet's critical friends, he altered it to Lugar, but there was nothing of poetic fire or fancy associated with " the moors and mosses many O " when the neighbouring feudalists fell out !

The two families in question were the Auchinlecks (or Afflecks) and the Colvills, and they were at one time on the most friendly terms, as behoved such close neighbours.

The home of the Auchinlecks and the castle of the Colvill family stood on opposite sides of the river, and so intimate were they that a rope provided a means of communication between the two, messages and letters being thus exchanged.

And then one day the neighbours quarrelled over some trivial matter, and intercommunication ceased.

Auchinleck, with savage humour, or failing to realise the consequences of his ill-timed joke, one day gave the signal that a communication was being dispatched to the enemy stronghold.

It took the form of a small parcel, and was duly sent along the rope and taken to Colvill to whom it was addressed.

The haughty old gentleman received it with

surprise, but his curiosity soon changed to rage when he discovered the contents—the remains of a sheep's head off which his correspondent had that day dined !

Calling his retainers he gained access to the enemy stronghold, and slew his one-time friend and neighbour.

The matter did not end there, however. Auchinleck was sib to the house of Douglas, and that redoubtable warrior could not brook such an insult to his blood.

Soon the Douglas faction were knocking at the Colvill door, and ere long the castle was a smoking ruin and the owner a prisoner. Why the Douglas burdened himself with the captive I do not know, but apparently he changed his mind on their ride home, and Colvill was summarily slain.

The Tethering of the Sow was an affair of an altogether different complexion—battle for the sheer joy of conflict.

For generations a blood feud, bitter in its intensity, had existed between the great Ayrshire families of Craufurd and Kennedy. Many attacks and counterattacks, forays and personal exploits had passed between the rival houses.

One day, in the far-off fifteenth century, a herald or scion of the Bargany Kennedys made his way to Kerse, the home of the Craufurd chief, then an old man whose fighting days were past.

His message to Kerse was that on a certain day the Kennedys would tether a sow on the Craufurd lands, and not all the armed might of that proud family could remove it !

Such were the times that it is needless to state the challenge was accepted with alacrity, and so Kyle and Carrick were again to measure strength.

Each side called up its hardy warriors and every preparation was made, the Kennedys to defend the sow they carried to the tryst, the Craufurds to drive it out of their domain and avenge the insult offered to their name.

The fateful morning arrived and the struggle began. All day the battle raged, and before night-fall the Craufurds drove the aggressors and their sow from their lands, each side suffering heavy losses.

Honour was satisfied—and the sow was " flitted " !

Think of the bloodshed and bitter hate en-gendered over a sheep's head displayed in ridicule—or the tethering of a sow on a certain piece of land on the longest summer day, with the taunt that the other faction could not " flit it." Puerile they seem to us now, but men played that game in the days when war was a ploy.

The story of the Westlands is one long tale of such deeds and encounters, foolish in modern eyes, but the real adventure of life in the times when spear and prowess alone protected house and name.

But where is there no trace of war or feud in this old land of ours ? No man need go far afield in quest of old romance—he can find it in full measure at his very door an he will.

Scarce a furlong from my own window lies a battle-field—a turning-point in Scotland's stormy history, for there a queen lost her throne, and with it her head.

All around, the street- and place-names are commemorative of the event and of those who took a part on that fatal day.

Here it was that the Regent Moray forever blighted the hopes of his half-sister, the ill-fated Mary Queen of Scots, who flits across the pages of our history with a wan and ghostly attraction. Had Mary but fled to France while the way was open instead of delivering herself up to the English warden, many a fell chapter would never have been written.

One of the streets hereabouts, with a peculiar irony, is named Lochleven Road, and mayhap few of the citizens dwelling there give a passing thought to the nomenclature of their neighbourhood and the how and why of it all.

What a wealth of romance and incident clings to the older Glasgow streets; what stirring tales could be told of the surroundings, now busy and populous suburbs.

And here is one of note!

Near-by, on the south-east, still stand the ruins of Cathcart Castle, hidden now by tall tenement buildings, past which clang electric cars; a district busy with the rush of everyday affairs, but perpetuating at its street corners the names and deeds of other days when the sword was mightier than the pen, and personal daring brought greater reward than do stocks and shares!

History tells us that from this old castle Mary gazed anxiously from a window, following the fortunes of her gallant little army until she saw her hopes forever blasted and her prospects melt like mist on the distant Ben Lomond.

The story that Mary viewed the battle from a window in Cathcart Castle is not merely possible, but indeed probable. Sir Walter Scott, however, definitely tells us that she " beheld this final and fatal defeat from a castle called Crookstane," but had that been possible all the incidents would require to be recast, as the reputed battle-field could not have been witnessed from Crookston.

Perhaps Scott confused Cathcart and Crookston, because at this latter Mary and Darnley are supposed to have spent their honeymoon. What a tragic bit of history it all forms ! Crookston, now also lending its name to a growing suburb, had many adventures in its time, and was besieged in the old feudal days, Mons Meg being dragged thither to add force to the argument.

Face west and pass Camphill — only a year or two since and it was a mask of wild hyacinths, known as " the Bluebell Wood," but now a crowded suburb—and you will come by Seton Avenue, in turn leading to Maitland and Lethington Avenues, each name significant, but now, like an old moss-grown milestone, meaning little to the fast-moving world.

Men gave all—and willingly—when they fought for lost causes in those days. Lord Seton for the part he took was forced to flee to the Continent, and was reduced to such straits that he acted as a common waggoner before his ultimate rehabilitation and return to Scotland.

Go a step farther and you are in Crossmyloof, a strange name for a city suburb, but one with a romantic traditionary origin.   The story is probably quite without foundation, but it is not devoid of interest.

When Mary's leaders found themselves out-generalled and out-numbered by Moray, they advised caution, and indeed delayed in forcing the issue.

With that impatience which was such a marked characteristic of her race, the Queen insisted in putting the issue to the trial.   When her councillors remained obdurate, Mary took from her bosom a crucifix, and placing it upon her open palm said : " As sure as this crucifix crosses my loof I shall this day brave the Regent."

The Queen's Park marches with Crossmyloof, and opposite was the Moray Park, a vacant space now also covered with suburban dwellings.

Strathbungo, slightly north, finds its origin, or rather its appellation, from a much older circumstance. It is, or at least so I have been told, a corruption of Strathmungo, because Glasgow's Patron Saint approached what is now the city from that direction, crossing over towards the eastern district where the Cathedral now stands, and his old-time pathway is now that busy district Crosshill.

And so within a square mile or two out of the many, we have tracks and traces of Saints and Kings, Queens, Regents and Warriors.

The tall old elms which blank my library window have witnessed many changes, but even they had not broken the ground until centuries after St Mungo had passed, so far back in the annals of time lies the origin of the city !

But the low-lying stretch of green hills which

form the distant background to the view must have witnessed it all, and more if they could only tell.

The call of the hills is strong in the blood of most true Scots. I know a man who comes from Argyll, a keen business man, immersed in affairs of importance six days of the week, but when he goes out of an evening to take the air, his footsteps lead to a high-lying part of his suburb from whence he can look out over the Clyde valley to the distant hills of home. The hills call to him, stir something in his blood, the feeling Stevenson expresses so finely in the lines :

> Be it granted me to behold you again in dying,
> Hills of Home.

Glasgow is ringed by hills, Highland and Lowland. Her story and traditions are linked and intermingled, and the whig and wearer of the tartan have equal share in her fame and achievements.

If the south road leads to the land of Wallace and the Bruce, on the west the Highland line entices and the heather hills beckon from many quarters.

In the West lie the silent lochs and the great bens, where red tartan warred with green, and the lonely glens are haunted by the deeds of past years. There Rob Roy held his own by the power of his blade, and from the same hill-sides was taken the gentle Cameron, last man to suffer for his part in the 'Forty-Five. Before his day the Clan Gregor, the Campbells, Macfarlanes and Colquhouns slaked their vengeance and righted their wrongs all independent of the King's writ ; Montrose harried

Argyll, and a man's tartan was his passport or his snare.

And so to-day when the sun is mounting and the birds are mating, when the dead bracken is still clinging to the slopes, either you cannot understand or your blood will tell you why Masefield sang :

It's the white road westwards is the road I must tread,
To the green grass, the cool grass, and rest for heart and
     head,
To the violets and the warm hearts and the thrushes' song,
In the fine land, the west land, the land where I belong.

II

ON THE ROAD TO INVERSNAID

Follow the road to the great wide spaces,
  Where high in the corries the free winds play;
There you will find in the distant places,
  Peace at the close of day.

EVERY morning a little robin comes and sings his matins at my bedroom window. Shrill, yet sweet, but not by any means a song of peace or goodwill. Indeed, a more pugnacious little rebel amongst his feathered peers I have yet to meet.

When his notes are expended he cocks his head to one side, looks into the room with the cheekiest expression imaginable, and seems to say : " Was not that effort worth a crumb or two of comfort ? "

On this morning I did not see him, although I left his reward as usual on the window-sill. It was too glorious an awakening to be abed, and so I was up and on the road to Inversnaid before Master Robin Redbreast had left the snug seclusion of the ivy, or wherever his dormitory retreat is to be found.

Soon I was past the last suburban outpost and under the open sky, but early as I was, the plough-boy had forestalled me, and the glistening black furrows bore plenteous testimony of his slow-footed industry.

Gradually I was reaching higher country, and behind me the smoke-pall of the great city was growing more evident as it hung, sullen-like, in the distance.

The air was sweet with the scent of burning wood as I passed through Drymen village. The cottage chimneys were smoking, and a farm-cart rattling along the Balmaha road showed that the world was about its business again.

Back there, under that distant Glasgow reek, I am a member of a club, where on the smoke-room fireplace there is carved the motto, " Gang Warily," and idly I wondered to myself if the busy clubmen who took their midday *aperitifs* there knew the origin of the phrase.

The motto " Gang Warily " links this quiet little village and the busy man's club through a long line of good swordsmen in the Drummond family.

The story is that " Maurice, son of George, son of Andrew, King of Hungary, being in command of the vessel in which Saint Margaret, afterwards Queen of Malcolm Canmore, embarked for Hungary, happened to be driven by storm into the Firth of Forth. Here, on landing, fortune befriended him, for he was made Steward of Lennox, and received from the hand of Malcolm the lands of Drymen, or Drummen, from which was derived the name of Drummond."

Five generations later we find one Sir John Drummond of Drummond, Thane of Lennox ; and his son, Sir Malcolm, obtained from King Robert a grant of land in Perthshire for his great services in the Battle of Bannockburn, where, by his advice, caltrops were first used as a defence against the

English horsemen. In memory of this wise counsel, as Burke informs us, " his descendants bore caltrops upon a compartment of their arms, along with the motto, ' Gang Warily.' "

Loch Lomond and her myriad charms are now in the rear, and away on the right are the hills which seem to circle Stirling like a rampart.

The bog myrtle—the badge of the Campbells—flourishes in profusion, and on rubbing a few leaves upon the palms of the hands, the scent is delicious and refreshing.

Suddenly there is a fleeting glint of silver from the Lake of Menteith, the only lake in this land of lochs and dark waters. Well it is that the very name should be singular and a thing apart, an association black in the record of our land ; for Menteith it was who betrayed Wallace to his enemies and later just missed ensnaring the Bruce in Dumbarton Castle.

It is told that a Menteith once sent his butler for a fresh supply of wine, so that his guests might not be in want. As this worthy was passing the lake he espied two well-known witches, each mounted on a bulrush by the water's edge. They hailed the butler, and he, honest man, mounted a bulrush alongside them, and was immediately transported to France !

He had sufficient presence of mind to hold on to the empty wine-cask through it all, and on suddenly finding himself inside a royal palace, he nimbly filled the cask with the most exquisite wine from the King's sideboard. It is pleasing to note that he also brought home a silver cup engraved with the Bourbon fleur-de-lys, and still more gratifying to learn that Menteith's guests pronounced the wine excellent.

There was a Graham—Sir John—known by the soubriquet " Sir John with the bright sword," said to be an ancestor of the Grahams of Gartmore, bordering on Aberfoyle. He built the Castle of Kilbride, which remained in the possession of his representatives, the Earls of Menteith, for almost two centuries. The Menteith Grahams were for long known by the " by-name " of " The Grahams of the Hens."

Tradition tells us that when the Stewarts of Appin, led by Donald Nan Ord, or Donald of the Hammer, were retreating from Pinkie they passed the Lake of Menteith and stopped at the house of the Earl. A marriage feast was in preparation, the principal dish being poultry, and the hungry Stewarts calmly appropriated the food. They were pursued and overtaken, when a fierce conflict ensued, in which the Earl of Menteith and most of his followers were slain, while it is said that Donald Nan Ord escaped with only one follower. From that date the Menteiths were known as the Grahams of the Hens.

Donald the Hammerer finished his days, full of remorse and regret, as a monk in Iona.

For all his wild life of pillage and bloodshed, the deed which led to his withdrawal from the scenes of his prowess was one committed in error.

When an infant, Donald owed his life to an old foster-mother who tended and looked after him when his parents were slain and his patrimony forcibly taken possession of by one Green Colin of Dunstaffnage.

Donald, for all his warrior ways, never forgot his humble benefactor, and in her old age presented her with a farm where she might end her days in peace and comfort.

One day the Hammerer observed his son doing some work or other on the farm, and incensed that one of his blood should so demean himself as to engage in manual labour, he drew his sword and in great fury advanced towards the young man with the intention of slaying him.

The son fled before his incensed sire, but Donald followed him into the farm-house. Seeing someone lying on the bed, and assuming in his rage that it was his son, he plunged his blade into the body, only to find that he had slain the old foster-mother to whom he virtually owed his all. And so in remorse Donald of the Hammer withdrew from the scenes of his tumultuous life and died in holy office.

Pleasing thoughts these to help one along this uninteresting highway, and then suddenly, as it were, the long straight road comes to an end. Over the little bridge at Gartmore Station, where, this morning, the Forth is ringed by feeding trout—great fellows if the monster glimpsed as I passed is a criterion—round the corner, and Aberfoyle lies below in a curious haze, part smoke, part mist.

A town of great traditions this, open enough to all to-day, but a spot which filled Bailie Nicol Jarvie's heart with nervous dread one morning in the long ago.

Then, as now, Aberfoyle stood as an outpost

betwixt the rich Lowlands on one side—on the other
the hills and lochs where the word of a Highland
chieftain carried greater weight than did ever edict
from the Crown Officers in Edinburgh.

But to those who know its secret, Aberfoyle is an
ancient stronghold of more than red tartan and
caterans. It is a haunt of the fairies.

But Scott was not quite accurate when he wrote :

> 'Tis merry, 'tis merry, in Fairyland
>   When fairy birds are singing ;
> When the court doth ride by their monarch's side,
>   With bit and bridle ringing.

For it is not always merry in Fairyland. Many
years ago Loch Lomondside was a famous rendezvous of the Sleagh Maith, or the Good People
as they were called by those careful not to give
offence. But a lazy, wicked curmudgeon of an old
man drove them from the bonnie banks by his
greed.

This is the true story of his ill-timed act. For
although the fairies are never seen nowadays on
Loch Lomondside, at one time they dwelt there,
and good kind fairies they were too, until frightened
or subdued by the bad-tempered old farmer who
had a croft not far from Inverbeg.

Here was a burn, and on the bank the fairies used
to hold their revels. But it was not all fun and
light-hearted dancing either, because at certain
seasons the hill-folk brought their wool of an evening and, wishing a wish as to the colour they would
like it tinted by the fairies, went off to bed. Sure
enough next morning the wool was always nicely

sorted and dyed as desired, and the honest farm-folk and the good fairies lived in undisturbed amity.

One day the old man referred to gathered all his soiled, dirty, matted wool, and without washing it or doing anything to help lighten the fairies' task, he dumped it all down at the burn-side, and in a loud grumbling voice ordered the fairies to bleach the wool pure white or he would make it hot for them !

Next morning his wool was beautifully white and clean, but so heavy had been the task and so frightened were the fairies that never again were they seen on Loch Lomondside, and so the Colquhouns must dye their own wool like other folk to this day !

Perhaps these disappointed little folks when they fled in their distress sailed across the loch to Aberfoyle, quite a long journey for such elfin-folk, carrying their queen in a fairy litter. But be that as it may, Aberfoyle has more than one fairy knowe and ring where high revels are held in the light of the harvest moon, the while seven little pipers make merry and the dancing thrives apace.

> And now they throng the moonlight glade,
>   Above, below, on every side,
> Their little minim forms arrayed,
>   In all the tricksy pomp of fairy pride.

Mortal eye has not seen them in our time, so far as I know, but they were familiar to the Rev. Mr Kirk, who flourished in the latter part of the seventeenth century. He wrote an intimate book on their customs and affairs, and was, in just retribution for disclosing their secrets, carried off by them to Fairyland in the end !

In this queer old volume he described even their food, and, of course, like all mortals who interfere and disclose such secret manners and rituals, they got him at last !

A queer tale it is—and a true one if the one-time gossip of the old clachan, now a ruin, is to be believed.

This reverend gentleman must have lived a full and busy life, and apart from his researches into the lives and habits of fairies, he was a proficient Gaelic scholar, insomuch that he went to London to superintend the printing of the Bible in that tongue. It was translated under the direction of Bishop Bedel, and was published about 1685.

His book on fairies, elves and other supernatural creatures was issued in 1691, under the title, " An Essay on the Nature and Actions of the Sub-terranean (and for the most part) Invisible People, heretofore going under the name of Elves, Faunes and Fairies, etc."

Fairies, according to this gifted authority, pos-sessed " light and changeable bodies of the nature of a condensed cloud."

In the course of his investigations he discovered their homes " in little hillocks, and here they are sometimes heard to bake bread, strike hammers and do such-like service."

The fairy-folk do not appear to reside per-manently in one hillock; indeed, for some reason which must be more deeply seated than mere restlessness, they move their habitat every three months or so, and during these migrations they may be seen by those gifted with second sight.

c

Mr Kirk relates a remarkable instance of two women who, unknown to each other, dreamed of some treasure buried in a certain fairy hillock. Not merely did they dream, but to strengthen their belief, voices directed them where to search. Proceeding to the appointed spot, they met and jointly discovered a vessel full of money, and dividing the spoil between them, as it was a time of famine, they were so enabled to buy grain. This was certainly good work on the part of the little people.

But Mr Kirk delved too deeply into those secret ploys, and the fairies bided their time and turned the tables on him. They came upon him, I take it, when he was ill-prepared to defend himself against their magic.

Scott was more accurate this time when he wrote the verse :

> It was between the night and day,
>   When the Fairy King has power,
> That I sank down in a sinful fray,
> And, 'twixt life and death, was snatched away,
>   To the joyless Elfin bower.

The truth is, it was evening, and the clergyman was walking upon one of these fairy mounds, situated not far from his manse, I trust, because he was dressed only in his nightshirt, when he suddenly sank in a swoon. The unenlightened took this for death, but the knowing ones averred that it was produced by the supernatural influence of the much-violated fairy people.

They buried him in Aberfoyle kirkyard, but

later he appeared " as a form " to a friend and told him of his awkward position, furthermore stating that only Graham of Duchray could restore him again to his friends in the mortal sphere, and he explained that at the baptismal ceremony of his posthumous child he would appear in the room, when Graham of Duchray was instantly to throw his dirk over his apparition, and he would at once be restored to his mortal form. True to promise, the spectral apparition materialised at the ceremony, but so astonished was Duchray that he altogether omitted to throw the dirk, with the result that Mr Kirk is still held in thrall by the fairies, whose tricks he did so much to expose !

But the minister of Aberfoyle occasionally took part in more stirring affairs than even the tracking and outwitting of elves and fairies.

One local affray at least was conducted in the presence not merely of the parish minister, but also of the elders.

The Earl of Airth, being anxious to serve certain papers upon Graham of Duchray, and finding, like many another man in these days, that it was one thing to obtain authority from the Court, but another matter to enforce it, learned that Duchray's son had arranged to have a child baptized on a certain date.

Assuming, and rightly, that Graham in person would be present at the ceremony, the Earl gathered his friends and retainers and escorted one, Mushat, the attendant messenger-of-arms, to the spot.

The Duchray party were crossing the old bridge

as the Earl's party arrived on the scene, and not wishing to precipitate matters, the messenger, with his own attendants, advanced towards Duchray and informed that gentleman that he must consider himself under arrest.

Without further ado the baby was set upon the ground, and the Duchray faction drawing swords and pistols, informed Mushat that those of the Earl's party who were not killed would be drowned in the river, and so pressed to the attack.

No great damage was done, although one or two of the Airth men were wounded, one man losing two fingers, while in sequel Graham of Duchray was bound over to keep the peace with the Earl and his tenants.

However, to revert to the fairies ere we leave their familiar haunts, another approved authority, one Martin by name, gives intimate details of the " men of peace " or fairy denizens of this district.

His pronouncements, if he may be accepted as an authority, and he writes with weight, are sadly against all my preconceived notions of fairyland.

Ponder well on these words if you are ever tempted to change your state for the more ethereal realm of elfland : " The *Daoine Shi*, or men of peace of the Highlands, though not absolutely malevolent, are believed to be a peevish, depressing race of beings, who, possessing themselves but a scanty portion of happiness, are supposed to envy mankind their more complete and substantial enjoyment. They are supposed to enjoy, in their subterraneous recesses, a sort of shadowy happiness—a tinsel grandeur ;

LOCH LOMOND FROM ABOVE ARDLUI

INVERSNAID PIER—GLEN ON OPPOSITE SHORE LEADS TO LOCH SLOY

which, however, they would willingly exchange for the more solid joys of mortality."

He too, like our ministerial friend, the Rev. Mr Kirk, gives full particulars of their abodes, and tells how many people were afraid to pass their homes beside Lochcon—on our road to-day—after sunset.

He tells how, if anyone is daring enough to go alone on Hallow-eve and walk round one of the fairy hills nine times towards the left hand, a door shall open and he may enter the subterraneous abode. Many have done so and been sumptuously entertained and regaled with choice and delicate viands and rare wines. Furthermore, the lady fairies " surpass the daughters of men in beauty."

Ever, then, take my advice and have nothing to do with it—there is always a snag somewhere, cropping up when the prospect seems fairest, and true it is : " But unhappy is the mortal who joins in their joys, or ventures to partake of their dainties. By this indulgence he forfeits for ever the society of men, and is bound down irrevocably to the conditions of a *Shi'ich*, or man of peace."

But even then, worse is to follow. Our author tells of a woman who carried out the prescribed formula and was admitted to the " secret recesses." There she met many mortals now held in thrall and powerless to escape. One of these transformed semi-humans, if I may so name them, warned this adventurous person of her fate, and advised her to abstain from eating and drinking for a certain period ; when her fairy hosts would lose their power over her and she would be released and sent back to join her fellow-mortals.

This advice she followed, and so in due time she found herself back on earth. Apparently she had retained what the Scots call her " grippin' senses," because on being restored she had brought with her the food she wisely abstained from consuming. Let me add, " When she examined the viands which had been presented to her, and which had appeared so tempting to the eye, they were found, now that the enchantment was removed, to consist only of the refuse of the earth."

All of which only goes to prove that fairyland is no better than it should be, and I for one intend to leave its fascinating people alone and unvisited.

Sir Walter Scott stayed at Aberfoyle for a time, gathering data for his " Rob Roy." Indeed, they say "The Lady of the Lake" was originally to find its setting here, but the minister, his host, was busy on a history of the district, and with his native courtesy Scott moved his plot to Loch Katrine.

It may not be true, but the lady who gave me the story was quite indignant against the minister for taking this extra glamour and romance from her beloved country-side !

No district which acted as the stage for the exploits of such a picturesque figure as Rob Roy MacGregor need feel the pangs of jealousy. His fame is as firmly fixed as is old Creagh Mhor himself, with one eye on the clachan and the other on Jean M'Alpine's, keeping guard betwixt and between with his head in the clouds and his feet in the Forth.

Even Wordsworth wrote a stave to his memory,

and compared him with his southern counterpart, Robin Hood :

> A famous man is Robin Hood,
> The English ballad-singer's joy !
> And Scotland has a thief as good,
> An outlaw of as daring mood ;
> She has her brave Rob Roy !
> Then clear the weeds from off his Grave,
> And let us chant a passing stave
> In honour of that hero brave !

The old clachan, or what is left of it, lies behind the main road, and the modern houses and shops quite conceal the traces of that former generation from the passer-by.

Once past Loch Ard, and on leaving behind the clustering villas which form the west-end of Aberfoyle, there is suddenly revealed the real West Highland beauty. On either side are hills and woods, the narrow road winding beautifully amid scenery painted at this season with lavish colours.

The russet-brown of the bracken, with here and there purple patches of the hard-dying heather, the whole view a patchwork of red, gold and brown, crimson and green. Dame Nature paints with a wonderful palette in Scotland, and nowhere more picturesquely than amongst the hills and glens.

A little farther on is an old mill. Tired and faded it looks this bright morning, like an ancient who has spent his days in hard work and craves to sit with weary, half-closed eyes and watch the younger world bustle past.

To the right, a few paces up the hill-side, is all that now remains of the inn where Bailie Nicol

Jarvie put up such a valorous show with a red-hot poker.

Many a plot would be hatched in Jean M'Farlane's Inn over a glass of usquebaugh, innocent of duty. A muttered warning in Gaelic, and the red tartan was off again to replenish that ever-aching maw of Rob and his freebooters.

Not so very long ago, if my memory serves me aright, a very old man lived in this ancient rickle of stones. There was no chimney, and the peat-reek escaped by the door—no very comfortable dwelling-place. He had some small fame as a breeder of dogs, and looked for all the world like a man who might have the second sight. But to-day the place knows him no more.

On passing Loch Chon, shining like a silver mirror in the morning sun, and studded with lovely green islets, on the right, some hundred yards or so from the highway, an old bridge, surrounded by tall bracken, spans the mountain burn.

It is well worth the time spent in diverging from the path for a moment or two, for this is a General Wade bridge, the work of that industrious law-keeper who made so many roads and opened up so much of the then untrodden lands. The centre or keystones have been removed, I suppose to prevent its further use now that the king's highway runs clear alongside, but even now the hill-track, for it is nothing more, winds away across the mountain-sides, a lasting tribute to the toil and sweat which created it.

I remember once an old shepherd pointing out the ruin of an ancient bridge on what was for

generations the main road from Girvan to Ballan-
trae. Here again, to deter anyone from still using
it, the keystones had been removed, and so well
was it built that it took the roadmen two days to
dislodge the first stone !

A great man General Wade, pioneer of hill-roads
and Patron Saint of those who explore the land of
mighty bens and dark lochs.

The other day I was reading about Wade, and
my author claimed that the kilt, as we know it
to-day, was invented or originated by an army
tailor who accompanied the General's forces in
Scotland in 1719 !

Back to the main Inversnaid road again, and soon
is reached a cluster of dwellings, surely ill-assorted
neighbours, yet blending wonderfully with their
setting. The tin house amongst the trees is the
manse, and on the right is a whitewashed farm-
house, quiet and peaceful in the morning sun, on
the spot where once frowned the Garrison of
Inversnaid, erected to keep the lawless MacGregors
in their place ! Here, perched on a little knoll,
in the heart of a beautiful Highland glen, stands
all that now remains of the old fort. Wolfe, afterwards famous for his victory at Quebec, was in
command.

The ruin, whose walls are some three feet in
thickness, is now used as a sheep-pen, one half
filled with cut bracken from the near-by hills.

Alongside is the old burial-place of the soldiers.
Deep sunk under the grassy moss, only the tops of
the stones are visible. Gone are the records of
the men who held the fort against the kilted out-

laws, and the only stone decipherable—and soon it, too, will fade under stress of weather—is that erected by the Duke of Montrose, that implacable enemy of the Rob Roy faction.

The inscription reads :

ERECTED

BY

THE DUKE OF MONTROSE

TO THE MEMORY OF THE

NON-COMMISSIONED OFFICERS AND MEN

OF THE

2nd, 3rd, 4th, 12th, 13th, 14th, 15th, 16th, and 17th, 19th, 20th, 21st, 23rd, and 31st and 43rd Regiments, who died while on duty at Inversnaid Garrison 1721–1796.

> And though no stone may tell
> Their name, their work, their glory,
> They rest in hearts that loved them well,
> They grace their country's glory.

Above the disappearing gravestones in this old God's acre, where literally " heaves the turf in many a mould'ring heap," are to be found, amongst other modern appurtenances, a hen-coop and a child's swing !

On my return through the glen I carefully picked a beautiful little fern from the garrison wall, for soon the few remaining traces will be gone, and its memory will live only in tradition.

Wolfe, who commanded here for a spell, was an honoured enemy. No man in the Hanoverian army was held in higher esteem. At Culloden, Wolfe refused to shoot the wounded clansmen ; in fact, tendered his commission rather than do so.

So perhaps the Heights of Abraham were won on Drumossie Moor in the generous hearts of his Highland heroes!

Just before coming to the deep descent which leads straight down to the loch-side, and the hotel which now adorns the spot where Rob Roy had his home, stands the beautiful little kirk with its wonderful stained-glass windows.

There is a strange little outside tower here with the kirk bell suspended, and every Hogmanay, just on the stroke of twelve, the elder (who is also church officer and sexton in one) rings a merry peal to tell the few scattered inhabitants and the startled deer that another Good New Year is being born to a glad world at peace.

And then when night fell, as I stood at the hotel door, the moon forming a silver pathway across the loch, the everlasting hills ringing me round and the breeze carrying the softly-whispered secrets from tree to tree, the world's turmoil seemed very far away.

Suddenly among the bracken there was a scream so human that for a moment it startled me. What it was I know not. Perhaps a rabbit with a weasel on its trail, perhaps the shouts of the Macfarlane ghosts from that ancient fort on Inveruglas Isle, still turning its empty sockets on Rob Roy's Cave. And then again silence.

As I stood there I thought for a moment of the many feuds this place had seen—of the Bruce—of Rob Roy and the wild clansmen who peopled it in bygone days. And then came to my memory a quotation from Jerome's " Three Men on the

Bummel." Here are the exact words, judge if they fit :

"In this land of many ruins, that long ago were voice-filled homes, linger many legends, and here again, giving you the essentials, I leave you to cook the dish for yourself. Take a human heart or two, assorted ; a bundle of human passions—there are not many of them, half a dozen at most ; season with a mixture of good and evil ; flavour the whole with the sauce of death, and serve up when and where you will. 'The Saint's Cell'; 'The Haunted Keep'; 'The Dungeon Grave'; 'The Lovers' Leap.' Call it what you will, the stew's the same."

When the drovers are returning from Glasgow, having delivered their charges to the buyers there, they come home to the distant west via Inversnaid, cross the loch by ferry, or landwise by Ardlui, and carry on straight as the crow flies across the hills. A hard, weary way it must be, but shortening the journey by half.

Mentally I journeyed with them by Ben Vorlich and Loch Sloy, and then, promising myself to follow in their path to-morrow, I turned my back on the still beauty of the night and went to bed.

GLENFALLOCH—THE ROWAN ROAD

III

LOCH SLOY

We are bound to drive the bullocks,
All by hollows, hirsts and hillocks,
Through the sleet and through the rain,
When the moon is beaming low,
On frozen lake and hills of snow,
Bold and heartily we go.

Lifting the Cattle

MOST folks who know anything about Scotland, or at least about the beautiful, romantic Westland, have heard of Loch Sloy, but not many take the trouble to search it out, hidden away as it is in the bosom of the hills, with Ben Vorlich, Ben Ime and Ben Vane as rugged guardians.

When found, it is not an impressive sight, but perhaps that is because one must pass Loch Lomond or Loch Long to reach it, and it suffers by comparison. But if it is not enshrined in song like Loch Lomond, or open to adventurers by deep waters like her sister, Loch Long, Loch Sloy is embalmed in the history of a clan known in the annals of midnight raids and cattle-lifting exploits, who went into battle with its name upon their lips.

" Loch Sloy " was the rallying or battle-cry of the Macfarlanes in the old days when " lifting " cattle was a sport and a business combined, and this particular part of Scotland was never very safe for any man who wore an alien tartan.

Macfarlanes, MacGregors, M'Lachlans, Colquhouns, Campbells, not to mention one or two
neighbouring septs or clans, formed a fitting popu-
lation for the rough hill-side and loch-studded
country now bereft of its feudal excitements, but
still wild and untamed as Nature formed it.

The Macfarlanes have a " gathering " tune,
" Thogoil nam bó " or " Lifting the Cattle," while
their near neighbours, the MacGregors, rejoice in
one " Ruaig Ghlinne Freoine " or " The Chase of
Glen Fruin." Each has a tale which we shall see
about later.

This morning, when I set out in quest of Loch Sloy,
I went by Loch Lomondside, through the Colquhoun
country, some twenty miles of winding beauty, all
haunting vistas, too wonderful almost to be real.

There is another road past Dumbarton Castle,
the scene of so many stern encounters in bygone
days, up Loch Longside, past Arrochar, and thence
to Loch Lomond. It goes through a pass to-day
thronged with motor traffic, where of yore the
boats of Haco and his wild Norsemen were dragged
overland to spoil the Lomond homesteads, until then
considered safe from the raiding sea-warriors.

But reach it as you will, the first part of your
journey must take you for a mile or two alongside
the busy Clyde and past the Kilpatrick hills, where
even since the days of Bannockburn the citizens
paid a yearly tax to be protected from the wolves
which infested the district.

If there were wolves and thirsty claymores on the
land, the waterways were by no means safe. Indeed,
about the time of Cromwell's death, piracy was

rife hereabouts. There was one Glasgow pirate whose ship carried seven guns, and who lay at the mouth of the Clyde and robbed foreigners going to or coming from Ireland.

He took seven vessels in one week, and General Monk wrote the English Admiralty to " capture and clap him in some secure place." Whether they ultimately captured him I cannot say, but such a fearless rogue deserved at least to fall in fair fight on his own quarter-deck.

Morally, he does not seem to me to be more outrageous than the worthy Glasgow merchants who fitted out a privateer and sent her to harry the Dutch. The *Lion* by name, she was a great vessel of 60 tons burthen, manned by a crew of sixty, with five guns, also muskets, half-pikes and pole-axes. She captured several prizes and brought them in triumph to Port Glasgow.

Indeed, it was with relief that I left behind me the old bustling roadway of kings and merchants, and made for the still calm of the sanctuary of Luss.

Robert the Bruce it was, I think, who ordained this lovely spot a sanctuary—where no man carried warlike implements—later to be ignored in some blood feud when passions raged high.

When I reached the Fruin Water, a burn which to-day runs peacefully into the loch, I paused for a moment and let my mind travel back adown the years. Is there any other language which in a word paints a picture like the Gaelic ?

Unfortunately my knowledge is too sparse to enable me to enter that wonderland of the Gael and enjoy the mysteries which have been handed down for generations, but I believe the Fruin Water means the "water of sorrow."

Many generations ago two MacGregors were returning to their native glen and their way took them by Loch Lomondside. Darkness was approaching, they were tired and hungry, and so they killed a sheep and feasted ere moving on again with the rising of the sun.

The sheep was a black wedder with a white tail. When in the early morning a Colquhoun came upon the remains of their ill-gotten meal and raised the alarm, the MacGregors were pursued, captured, and ruthlessly hanged.

Sheep were plentiful enough, and the crime was not an unusual one had not ill-feeling between the tartans magnified the offence. It was an ill-deed for the Colquhouns, and brought a pitiless return on their clan.

When the MacGregors heard of this summary justice, as was to be expected, revenge was their urge, and for some forty or fifty years reprisals, raids and forays were the rule.

Following the hanging of their two clansmen, the MacGregors did not long ponder on their course of action, and shortly one, Patrick MacGregor of Leggarnie, carried off a herd of cattle from Luss.

The Macfarlanes appear to have joined blades with the MacGregors in their forays, and so from time to time the Colquhouns were made to realise that a blood feud was active.

But worse was to come. One February morning in the year 1603 the Colquhouns had advice from their spies or watchmen that a MacGregor force, some three hundred strong, was advancing towards Glenfruin. This time it was evident that the MacGregors meant no mere cattle-raiding escapade, but were intent on war to the knife, because they were led by their regular captain, Alastair MacGregor of Glenstrae. With them were some Macfarlanes and a few Camerons—fighting men all.

The Colquhouns at once took the field, probably nothing loth, led by Sir Alexander, their chief, but they were a poor match in strategy or warlike fervour compared with their opponents.

The defenders greatly outnumbered the MacGregors, their forces being some three hundred horse and four hundred foot, or fully two to one, but mere numbers were not to save the day.

The MacGregor divided his forces—one party allowing the Colquhouns to pass and attack what they understood to be the full enemy force, when they, in turn, fell on the enemy's rear. Soon the issue was joined, but the practised blades of the MacGregors quickly settled the affray in their favour. Great slaughter was done, and Loch Lomondside was ravaged and spoiled by the victorious avengers.

One man, Allan Oig MacAntuach, it is said, became so frenzied with blood-lust that when the Colquhouns had fled, he rushed upon a party of students and non-combatants who had assembled to witness the battle, and slaughtered some forty of them in cold blood.

There is more than one version of this incident, and there is perhaps doubt about it, but probably some untoward incident did take place. One of

D

the unarmed citizens said to have been murdered was a Tobias Smollett, a bailie of Dumbarton, and doubtless an ancestor of the novelist.

The victorious MacGregors drove off the cattle, sheep and goats, and harried the district thoroughly when they were at it, "with the haill plenishing, gudes and geir of the four-score-pound land of Luss, burning and destroying."

The Government of the day was harsh and cruel in their repression as a result of this affair. The very name MacGregor was proscribed. No minister could marry or baptize one of the name, and they were hunted and harried from place to place.

If any man outlawed for crime killed a MacGregor of equal rank, he obtained not merely a free pardon, but in addition a reward of a thousand pounds Scots. In this way was the majesty of the law upheld, and it was many years ere a MacGregor could openly pass under his own name and yet freely mix with his fellows. Many of them assumed other names— Stewart, Grant, Cunningham, Drummond, and so on—but through it all,

MacGregor despite them shall flourish for ever !

Scott, in whose words so much Scottish national history is enshrined, by whose pen so many otherwise forgotten incidents are recorded, puts the following stirring lines into the mouth of one of the clansmen :

Proudly our pibroch has thrilled in Glenfruin,
    And Bannachra's groans to our slogan replied ;
Glen Luss and Rossdhu, they are smoking in ruin,
    And the best of Loch Lomond lie dead on her side.

Widow and Saxon maid long shall lament our raid.
  Think of Clan Alpine with fear and with woe ;
Lennox and Leven-Glen quake when they hear again
  Rodreigh Vich Alpine dhu ho ieroe.

Matchless on the field of battle, the MacGregors were powerless against a schemer like Argyle, who now took a hand in the game. The MacGregor surrendered, and under promise of a safe-conduct across the border delivered himself to the honour of the Campbell chief. Argyle played him false, and once his treacherous word had been fulfilled and MacGregor was safely over the border, he was then arrested and brought back to execution in Edinburgh.

By virtue of his position as Chief, MacGregor was hanged his own height above his clansmen, eleven in number, but all twelve paid the last penalty on one gallows.

A curious incident is related in connection with this wholesale execution. A young Edinburgh citizen, by name James Hope, who was amongst the crowd witnessing the affair, suddenly fell down, having lost the power of his body. The real truth probably is that he took a shock, but he maintained that one of the Highlanders had shot him with an arrow.

It took a long spoon to sup with Argyle, and what his neighbours gained by prowess in the field they invariably lost in the council chamber.

To-day, under the genial sunshine in this smiling country-side, it is hard to think that such deeds of blood and evil were enacted not so very long ago as history reckons time, but such are the facts.

The calm ripple of the loch, the haunting aroma of peat-reek were far removed from war and slaughter.

Many a time I have puzzled at the miniature stacks of peculiarly-shaped wooden blocks which used to stand, built by a craftsman's hand, opposite a little cottage near-by this spot. More than once I have paused to look at them and wonder at their meticulous curves, in the belief that somehow they were used for salmon nets or something of the sort.

To-day the little stacks were gone, and on inquiry I was told that they were the handiwork of an old man, a survivor of the ancient craft of clogmakers, and that the wooden blocks were destined to make soles for Lancashire lasses !

Keen anglers tell me there is a peculiar species of fish which is only known to this loch. It is for all the world like a herring, and will not take the fly no matter how deft the fisherman may ply his rod.

The theory is that Loch Lomond was aforetime a salt-water loch, but some great cataclysm separated it from the sea, and so by degrees as the water became fresh the denizens gradually acclimatised themselves to the changed conditions. This I leave for geologists to decide, but I think it is correct to state that the bones of whales have been discovered near-by, and this adds colour to the theory !

Of course every Scottish loch has traditions of some sort, and one of those associated with the " bonnie banks " of Loch Lomond is that of a floating island ! Maybe it was on this island that a young M'Lachlan met with a mysterious end.

It appears he was on his way to Dunblane, and having dined at Inverbeg and being impatient for the ferry to take him across the loch, he built a huge fire on the foreshore. In response to the signal a beautiful maiden approached, but the M'Lachlan's companion, detecting something uncanny, refused to enter her boat.

Against his reason, but unwilling to be parted from his charge, he at last reluctantly took his seat. On approaching an island they heard beautiful music, and the M'Lachlan stepped ashore with his enchanter. A huge wave overturned the boat, and while his companion managed to cling to it and save his life, the daring young chieftain and his fairy bride disappeared, never to be seen again.

Superstition does not get much credence in these matter-of-fact days, but it has left us some wonderful tales and traditions.

Loch Lomond's near-by rival, Loch Katrine, has also some wonderful romance woven round the name. Indeed, the one-time valley which is now the loch was for long the home of a race " virtuous and wise." Ben Venue at this time possessed a well of pure spring water, much prized by the inhabitants, and the glen folks placed the well in charge of a young maiden named Katrine.

One evening, while employed in her task of guarding the well, a handsome young Highlander approached Katrine and gave her some cordial to drink to his health. The girl fell instantly into a deep slumber, and the winning young Highlander at once changed into his natural shape, that of a demon who haunted the mountain. He cut the sluices and the water rushed down the hill-side, drowning all the people in the valley.

On recovering from her trance, and observing the calamity her carelessness had produced, the maiden threw herself into the water, which from that day has been named Loch Katrine.

On dark winter nights the demon can still be heard shrieking and howling among the hills—but whether in sorrow at the results of his action or in fierce exultation at his misdeeds will never be known.

Almost every loch has some queer story or dark legend, more fitting as fireside tales than for this springlike morning when the snowdrops are nodding as I pass, and soon the banks will be a fairy-haunted mass of wild hyacinths. Primroses will ere long peep from under the bank, to give place in turn to tall, graceful fox-gloves, festooned in many varieties of moss and fern. How beautifully nature paints her canvas here at every season of the year !

As I paused for a moment to admire old Ben Lomond, still wearing a rakish white mutch although spring was in the air, I spied what at first glance appeared to be a mouse. Suddenly the stillness was broken by a shrill, stabbing trill, and then I knew my sudden visitant was a wren. A careless movement of my foot and the little brown songster disappeared as mysteriously as he came.

Earl Grey of Fallodon, that delightful authority on bird life, once said that he endeavoured never to let a month pass without hearing the wren sing. So clear, so defiant, so sweet a note has he, this tiny knight-errant of the hedgeside.

The wren has many associations, varying throughout Britain, but in some Highland districts there is a tale that he is greater than the eagle. One day the two birds had an argument as to which could soar highest, and the cunning wren perched unnoticed on the eagle's back.

Up went the king of birds, higher and higher, until the earth was far below. "Where are you now, Mr Wren?" he cried, exulting in his height and power. "Here," answered the wren, springing off his back and hovering above him.

Dryden puts the story in verse:

> Fool that I was! upon my eagle's wings
> I bore this wren, till I was tired with soaring.
> And now he mounts above me.

The golden eagle is not by any means extinct, and one forenoon, not so very long ago, a mother bird and two young sailed majestically over the town of Greenock. The mother had a large gull in her talons, and its moaning cry attracted attention.

Probably this prey was being taken alive to some hill-bound eyrie to serve as a cruel but necessary object-lesson in wild-craft to the youngsters before they, too, embarked upon their own adventurous careers.

Lunch-time thoughts grew urgent just as I arrived at Tarbet, and here the talk was of sport. A native had the previous evening shot a fox! Shades of Clan Macfarlane I was prepared to face (this was an apparent danger when molesting their old-time rallying place and hunting ground), but the ghost of John Peel was more than I could risk,

so after a hasty snack I was on the winding road
again, and now almost at the parting of the ways,
the point where the king's highway must be left
for the heather-clad sheep track.

A wild road this ; indeed, after the first mile or
so the pathway, which merely led to a lonely farm-
house, entirely disappeared.

Here on the bleak, bare track reads a notice
against fishing in Loch Sloy, signed by a Colquhoun
factor. "The world has many turns." How
obvious it is that the Macfarlanes are a broken clan
when trespass notices are erected on their old clan-
ground by the ancient enemy.

The notice served one good purpose at any rate.
It gave me assurance of being on the right way to
find the loch, as a more deserted, bleak landscape it
would be difficult to imagine. The hills were snow-
covered and the ground underfoot was mere bog.

On glancing back ere finally saying farewell to all
apparent animate life, I had a most enchanting view
of Inversnaid across the loch. Somewhere below
where I stood the Bruce must have landed with his
followers, some five hundred stout warriors.

After the Battle of Methven the Bruce and his
small army were making for Cantyre when they were
hard pressed by the MacDougalls, and in error found
themselves on the east side of Loch Lomond. They
had gone astray somewhere in Glen Falloch, and
now must cross the loch or be attacked by their
enemies.

Douglas, the King's lieutenant, had the good
fortune to discover an old leaky boat, but willing
hands soon patched it up and Bruce was first to

cross over. The boat held only three men, and so it took all night to transport them, but every one was safely landed.

To keep up their spirits, Bruce regaled his men with tales of chivalry, until the Earl of Lennox, coming unexpectedly upon the Scottish King and his followers, relieved their fast and pointed the way to safety.

Meanwhile I was squelching through peat and moss. The pathway had suddenly deserted me, unless that were it changed to a mountain burn, and there was not so much as a bird on the sky-line.

No sound but the ripple of water, and there was plenty of it and to spare. Here and there a wild-eyed sheep would suddenly emerge from among the huge rocks and boulders, look as if it were going to make vocal protest at my intrusion, and then as suddenly disappear into its native fastness.

The weather had altogether changed. The spring sunshine of an hour ago was gone, and the wind was bitter cold, and slowly it occurred to me that perhaps no such place as Loch Sloy actually existed.

A bad place to go astray on a dark night with more snow to come. Be it said, the Boots at lunch-time had given me careful instructions, but here was no living soul to guide or direct. Right in my path lay a sheep, dead, but what had gone wrong with the poor beast I could not tell. It had not been long dead, and while neither living bird or beast was in sight, the eyes had already been picked out, and the empty sockets gave it a ghastly, forlorn look! To pass I had to desert the path for a moment, to sink ankle-deep in peat moss.

Later I began to think that even if there were
such a loch, what good did it do me to get soaked
and tripped and chilled to see a sheet of water?
Still, on I went, and in due time came reward.
There lay Loch Sloy, screened by rocks and suddenly
breaking into vision. It was starting to snow again,
and a mist was coming down off the hills, and while
the distance from the main road is really nothing,
the going underfoot made it essential to get back
safely ere daylight departed.

> The evening mists, with ceaseless change,
> Now clothed the mountains' lofty range,
>   Now left their foreheads bare.
> And now the skirts their mantle furl'd,
> Or on the sable waters curl'd,
> Or on the eddying breezes whirl'd,
>   Dispersed in middle air.

In the strath somewhere near the loch a party
of Athole men were burned to death by a band
of Macfarlanes, under one Black Duncan. Hereabouts, too, the MacGregors were hunted with
hounds, and these dogs sometimes wore a light coat
of mail as a protection against arrows.

The Macfarlanes also carried on a feud with the
neighbouring Buchanans, and on one occasion one
of the latter was tortured for a long day before
being put to death. So that, taken all over, it
must have been an exciting environment for a
generation or two.

They were great cattle-lifters in their time, the
Macfarlanes. The full moon is even yet known
in the West as " Macfarlane's lantern," because by

its light the rievers got busy and drove bestial, which was wealth gained not by work or toil, but in a gentlemanly way pillaging one's neighbours, or the tempting near-by Lowlands.

To-day there is nothing to indicate life, past or present. No mournful cry of peesweep, not even the bleat of a sheep or the whirr of a grouse to break the bleak, awesome silence, and it was a relief to come abreast of the lonely little sheep farm again, and to find a dry path back to the roadway.

IV

TO CRIANLARICH—
THE ROWAN ROAD

So wondrous wild, the whole might seem
The scenery of a fairy dream.

Lady of the Lake

FROM the spot where the Uglas burn sings its merry farewell to the hill-side and loses its identity in Loch Lomond, the road is a sheer delight to every open-air sense.

I could quite as easily have tramped alongside Loch Sloy and come out somewhere near-by Ardlui, but it meant sacrificing the wonderful winding roadway with its beauties and its charm, and that could not be thought of.

Here, just where I deserted the hill-side for this panoramic roadway—for only so could I name it—is to be seen a most interesting example of the power of growth, the hidden, irresistible force of Nature. A huge rock weighing many tons has been split in two by a sturdy holly tree, which grows between the halves severed by the surprising and almost unbelievable strength of its roots.

Soon, too soon, so wondrous is its thrall, Loch Lomond will be passed, and over there a last glance reveals the rocky bank where Rob Roy's cave is hidden.

To-day the rocks haunted by spirits of the old-time clansmen are given over to the wild goats, and they, in truth, can be no more sure-footed than were the old-time Gregarach; no more wary of a strange footstep in their fastness.

An old friend who resides hereabouts offered me a kid as a pet, but it looked too much a creature of the wild to be taken from its natural environment; as well cage a golden eagle as hem such a creature from its free, untrammelled life, and I regretfully declined.

He informed me the goats were there, so many per farm, to protect the sheep from injury. Agile and sure-footed as wild cats, they delight to browse among the almost inaccessible rocks and crop the available verdure, and so remove the temptation for the sheep to adventure and perhaps come to grief! Whether this is usual or not I cannot say, but certainly it holds good in this quarter, and, moreover, adds still another picturesque touch to the story.

The black cattle, which formed the wealth of the rievers, the itch for which gave rise to so many daring forays, have to-day given place to the hardy sheep.

When the sheep began to invade the hill country, so little was their culture understood that a law had to be passed prohibiting the wool being *plucked* instead of shorn, indeed the ignorant, rather than definitely cruel, practice was quite a usual custom in some parts.

Just after passing the "dripping rocks," easily found by virtue of the water which eternally drips

down their face on to the roadside, we pass the
" Pulpit Rock." A glance at this curious stone is
not wholly without interest, but the gradual growth
of trees is shielding it from the public eye, and
in these days of speed many old-time landmarks
go unnoticed.

There are so many misty tales and traditions
about this rock that it is difficult to know just
what to believe. Some say it was in use during
the Covenanting period and that the minister of
Arrochar preached to his faithful flock, using the
peculiar pulpit-like cave, some four feet above the
ground-level, for this purpose. This might well
be, as the Macfarlane clan fought on the Moray
side against Mary Queen of Scots at the ill-fated
Battle of Langside, and later in the " Killing times "
there were many strange pulpits in use.

Of all the tales of the rock, the one I prefer
savours more of war, or rather of individual combat, and is older than any of them.

You can doubt it if you will, but some hundreds
of years ago a fierce black bull of Scotland met a
great red bull of England on the side of Ben Vorlich.
How that came about I cannot say, but you must
accept the fact on faith.

They engaged in mortal combat, and in the
course of this conflict of giants, the huge Pulpit
Rock was dislodged and sent tumbling down the
mountain-side. The Scottish bull overcame and
dispatched his English rival, but still sometimes
the knowing ones call the rock the Stone of the
Bulls.

Every autumn I pass along the loch-side road on

my way to Crianlarich to gather rowans, and all
this district is verdant with the graceful trees, so
beautiful at every season. The oak, the fir, the
silver birch are plentiful and wonderful in their
own way, but for me the rowan has always held a
fascination, a charm not merely for its graceful
beauty, but for its place in song and tradition.

Lady Nairne has immortalised it, and if no other
verse had ever been written, her words alone have
appointed its place in the heart of all lovers of this
fairest of our trees.

> Thy leaves were aye the first o' Spring,
> Thy flow'rs the simmer's pride ;
> There wasna sic a bonnie tree
> In a' the country-side.

That old song is known wherever a Scotsman
goes. What village lad did not find it part of his
Friday afternoon curriculum in the schooldays of
auld lang syne ? What if the beautiful simple
melody was slightly mutilated, enthusiasm for the
cause raised it above such petty considerations,
and its soul-haunting melody must often awaken
slumbering chords in the heart of many a wanderer.
And here is a profusion of the graceful tree—
miles of beautiful scenery made lovelier by its
presence.

Some say the Cross was fashioned of rowan, but
this I know, this tree brings good luck and wards
off evil spirits, and for this purpose it was planted
at cottage doors ; and so it is fitting that it should
flourish in dark glens and on sombre hill-sides.

If the rowan has a serious rival hereabouts it is

in the glistening evergreen holly which also abounds, but notwithstanding their prevalence in this district, neither has been adopted as the badge of a local clan.

That of the Macfarlanes is the cranberry; the MacGregors sport the pine; the symbol of the Colquhouns is the dogberry, and the Campbells have the sweet-scented bog myrtle.

How beautiful everything seems on a morning like this! The catkins give an added charm, and there is a very profusion of *yellow* bloom. Strange that Nature tends so much towards yellow at this season. The graceful daffodil, the shy primrose, sturdy whins, and every roadside starred with colt's-foot.

Some of the colt's-foot duly found its way into the vasculum, to be dried and held in readiness against the colds and chills of next autumn. A sovereign specific this for these common ailments, and one not appreciated as it deserves!

But now we are mounting, a happy lilting burn on the right, and Glen Falloch opens before us serene and perfect in its loneliness.

It was down Glen Falloch brave Bruce and his gallant little army came that day they missed the path and found themselves on the wrong side of the loch. And oftentimes since their day has this old glen given back the answering defiance as MacGregors followed their war-pipes, or Macfarlanes drove their lifted cattle at the run in the white moonlight.

Here, too, might be met from time to time Athole men in peace and war; Camerons, clansmen of more than one contending faction when

the Fiery Cross called them forth with claymore
and targe to redeem their wrongs or maintain their
rights. How many tired warriors have slaked their
thirst or bathed their wounds at that tumbling,
foaming hill-burn; to-day, as then, leaping in silver
cascades on the mountain-side ?

MacNabs, Campbells, Stewarts—what tartan has
not at one time or another used this silent sombre
pass to the Lowlands and the open world beyond ?

> As wild and as untamable
> As the rude mountains where they dwell.

Down the same glen one morning adventured
three Athole men on a private mission of vengeance.

They came to find one Duncan Dhu, and punish
him for the part he had taken when some of their clan
were burned in a hut by that warrior and his friends.

Coming upon a man splitting the trunk of a tree,
they questioned him about the whereabouts of this
Black Duncan, unaware that they were addressing
him in person.

Under promise of secrecy and reward, Duncan
agreed to point out their man if they would first
help him to complete his task.

The Athole men readily agreed, and the wily
Duncan requested them to hold the split portion
of the tree while he drove the wedge deeper. They
grasped the huge trunk, but instead of driving in
the wedge, Duncan, with an upward blow, released
it, and the trunk closed on the hands of the three
clansmen, holding them fast in a vice-like grip.
With a cry of exultation Black Duncan speedily
dispatched his enemies.

E

But if the day of feud and harry among men is over, Nature still carries on her ruthless ways. For a moment I stopped to watch a hawk, suspended like a huge spider, and then so sudden was its swoop that it was gone ere it seemed to move! On the right a trout leaped—a perfect beauty he was—and there was a fly the less in the world. Shortly a weasel, intent on some evil design be sure, ran with peculiar motion across the roadway and was lost in the stone dyke. If man has been tamed, fur and feather carry on the old savage pitiless quest, and war is still rife in this apparently quiet and peaceful glen.

Rowan trees guard the wayfarer all the while to Crianlarich, that village junction of the roads to the open spaces of the West. And here too, of an autumn afternoon, every approach, almost every cottage garden, is bright with the beautiful berries, and old Ben More must find his trusteeship an easy task with such wards of good fellowship flourishing at his feet.

From Crianlarich on, my trail is a secret one— for here, with three gallant companions, I go to camp—away from the dust and rush and strife of the outer world. So secluded is this haven among the hills, that for some seven or eight years the same derelict sheet of corrugated iron has acted as wind-screen for our fire.

On the right is a long, not too steep, hill-side; in the autumn afire with rowan berries, the scarlet hips of the dog rose, and purple heather. To-day the whins will be bursting into yellow patches and the background of last year's bracken will look like burnished bronze.

On the left is a rock-strewn hill, also with its gallant trappings of rowan, but here many years ago a huge wound was cut to supply whinstones for the road surface.

In front, the roadway takes a sudden turn, the trees step briskly into line, and the impression from even a few yards off is that a fir wood bars further progress.

It is here that we bivouac—in a small grassy depression at the side of the miniature loch, hidden from the few passers-by, and sheltered from the breeze by the tall Scotch firs.

The last mile always provides a tense moment or two. What if someone has chanced upon our spot to picnic, or even halt for an hour ? But no one ever has, and the fears surely are groundless.

Round the corner we go—and the first glance shows a flurry of blue-grey smoke, the pungent, sweet scent of a wood fire. The worst has happened, our fears are realised, someone has to-day forestalled us !

A man is using our corrugated sheet to stifle his fire before moving on. A yard or two down the road a woman with a child's perambulator, loaded only with personal effects, is waiting her lord's pleasure.

" Leave it, please," I shouted, running towards him ; " it will save us making a fire, and we'll camp here for an hour." In an instant the iron sheet was kicked aside, a handful of twigs from the plenty around, and the merry crackle was joy to our hearts.

Soon the kettle sings a merry tune and the lunch is spread and waiting. Delicious scones, gleaned from a farm kitchen on the journey, figure largely in the menu, and never did West End chef have more appreciative patrons. And then to lie back on the cut bracken and smoke with a contented mind—can life hold more, I wonder?

A damp, mossy bank on the loch-side is rich in peculiar fungus-like growths, brilliant crimson in colour, with black or white spots, and as large as tea-plates.

Someone told me this fungus grows and lives on dead matter, and that but for its development the fallen leaves would mount and increase until growth would be stifled. It may be so, and more every day is it brought home to me that Nature does nothing without a purpose; that everything is part of the mosaic we call life, ever changing but always working to a preconceived plan and pattern: however, to me their strange, vagrant beauty is excuse enough.

So clear is the water that by standing quite still for a moment we can see the lazy-looking trout moving about in aimless fashion, to whisk out of sight when a movement disturbs them.

But no one is here to molest their solitary domains, and as I moved away from the quiet little loch, with its dark mantle of firs, it was to leave it all to an undisturbed, almost primeval silence.

The winding path leads on to a land of mighty bens and deeper lochs: a land where great deeds found their stage in the years that are now but a memory; where the ready claymore was the arbiter between clan or sept, and prowess was the final judgment, and so, carefully extinguishing the embers of our fire, we took the North road.

LOCH LUBHAIR, GLENDOCHART

V

BY GLENDOCHART TO KILLIN

Here the war-pipes' music shrill,
  Strengthened thew and heart.
Echoed back the hills the wild refrain.
  Dark and lonely now the glen,
  Gone the gallant fighting men,
Still in loyal hearts their deeds remain.

As I left Crianlarich the air was redolent of scents sweet and haunting as a summer afternoon, and through it came a whiff of peat-reek, true indication of Highland lodgings.

Ben More stood gaunt and silent on the right, green with the coming of spring, and once again the roadway was a winding vista of charm and beauty, a lilting happy stream on the left, hills sloping away on the right, not dark and forbidding, but in the bright sunshine flashing signals of peace and goodwill when the rays scintillated on the snow patches which mosaiced the landscape on every side. In fact, genial as the morning was, bright and powerful the sun, snow seemed loth to lose its hold on the hill-sides, and clung precarious in the hollows and rocky clefts.

Loch Dochart springs suddenly into view as you come round the bend; to-day its only tenants one or two squalling gulls. There is good fishing here, as evidenced by the row of boats, a dozen or so, each chained to its post and awaiting " the gentle-man from London," or other sporting tenant.

But I had no eyes for fish this morning, although here and there one jumped clear in his exuberance. In the centre of the loch is a rocky, tree-grown island with the ruins of an old-time fortress standing staunch and upright, foursquare against all comers.

It was a Campbell retreat at one time ; indeed, if the tale is true, one of seven strong places in the possession of the Campbells of Loch Awe, built by Sir Duncan of that ilk.

This particular fortress, guarding its island site so arrogantly this peaceful morning, was supposed to be impregnable, and might well have been in some districts, but here MacGregors or MacNabs were not clans to sleep soundly when vengeance was still unslaked or wrongs called for redress, and so one night the MacGregors sacked it when the Campbells were in residence : a dear lesson on the advantages of keeping watch and ward when such dangerous clansmen were on foray.

It was winter, the loch was frozen, the oppor-tunity too golden to pass. The MacGregors crept silently across the ice-bound loch, no more than shadows from the sinking moon, surprised the fortress, and put all the inmates to the sword !

Great clansmen the Gregarach ; and even this morning, as I photographed the solid-looking old relic, the boat I stood in was named the *Rob Roy*. If there are any Campbell ghosts about, preserve me from fishing from a boat of that name some moon-light night ! Every owl in the woods above would make my heart leap, every rustle amongst the island trees bring sudden visions of Campbell vengeance on those who dared to embark on their territorial waters in a barque bearing a MacGregor name !

In the days of the great Montrose and his arch-enemy Argyle, this district was naturally in an uproar. The MacGregors and the MacNabs were for Montrose, and some Campbells, joined by Stewarts, Menzies and others invaded Glendochart to the number of fifteen hundred men. They ravaged the island keep and proceeded towards Strathample, where they laid siege to the castle, but retreated towards Menteith on the approach of the Athole men led by Graham and Drummond. The forces met near Callander, and some eighty of the invaders were slain ere they made good their escape towards Stirling.

Montrose himself passed through the glen on his way to carry terror and devastation to the Campbell lands of Argyle.

But wild nights and keen blades seemed far away this glorious morning. Beside me a bank of nestling velvety wild violets, and a very myriad of wood anemones growing in a rich soft carpet of moss and dainty little ferns, while the repeated, seemingly endless, call of the cuckoo—the first I have heard this year—echoed across the loch as clear as a bell. A droning old bumble-bee grumbled around for a moment or two, and an early squirrel kept a questioning eye on my movements for quite a time considering how busy he appeared to be ! I dallied here too long, but the silent beauty and charm of the place made it difficult to leave.

Again the winding, roundabout road, only an odd hundred yards visible at a time, but of itself so full of charm that one can spare the longer view.

Over behind those western hills, a road we do not traverse to-day, lies Dalree, intimately associated with an incident which might well have altered the whole history of our land.

The Bruce, you remember, slew the Red Comyn at Dumfries, and as that gentleman was related by marriage to the Lord of Lorn, Chief of the MacDougalls, that clan was inspired with an implacable hatred towards the King.

After hiding in the wild Athole and Breadalbane country with his almost dispirited army, now little more than three hundred men, the royal force was endeavouring to reach Argyle. Approaching Dalree they were attacked by Lorn, who had under him some thousand fighting clansmen. The odds against Bruce were too heavy, and he was forced to retreat, contesting every foot. Bruce was in the rear, and at length, coming to a narrow pass, the King, single-handed, guarded his men, who were now more certain of escape.

Three of the MacDougall faction, a father and two sons, determined either to slay or take their chief enemy prisoner. Bruce was mounted, and one of the sons grasped the rein, but the King killed him. The second of his attackers endeavoured, by grasping his leg, to unseat him, but his horse, being spurred, gave a forward bound and knocked his assailant to the ground ; as he rose Bruce struck him with such force as to cleave his head in two. The father, now desperate with fury at the death of his sons, grappled with Bruce and held him so closely that he could not wield his sword. Drawing a hammer which hung at his saddle, the Bruce struck and vanquished his third foe by dashing out his brains. Even then, the dying Highlander maintained his fierce grip, and the King had to unfasten his cloak to free himself, and thus the famed Brooch of Lorn fell into the hands of the MacDougall family.

Here again, the MacGregors, when fighting was afoot, had to play their part, and a band of that restless clan took part with the MacDougalls against the King.

Later, when power came his way, the Scottish King did not omit to collect his debt from the MacDougall faction, and to establish his sovereignty over his fierce vassals. He drove John of Lorn out of his country, and presented a considerable part of it to one Sir Colin Campbell, first of the feudal family of Argyle, a name destined to become known in many ways as the centuries passed.

The MacNabs, on whose clan ground we now are, also took part with the MacDougalls, and the Bruce paid them back in kind at a later date when his star was in the ascendant.

It is said these two clans took sides with the invaders against the Scots at Bannockburn, their hatred of the Bruce being stronger than their patriotism.

When leaving Crianlarich, if the south and west shoulders of Ben More were green and verdant, a backward glance revealed that his broad back was still white, and with the dying of the sun a snell wind would spring up.

Somewhere hereabouts a MacNab who had been out in the '45 was believed to be hiding, and the redcoats were sent to burn down his house. It was duly fired, but on moving off someone noticed that the flames were apparently extinguished. A man was sent back to re-kindle it, and MacNab, who had been on the watch and had quenched the flames, shot him dead. The soldiers rushed to take the outlaw prisoner, but three were shot before he was dislodged. Taking to the rocks, he managed to account for a further three, when the soldiers retired, and for the time being, at least, left him in possession.

The same wise old hills look down on us to-day, storied in tales we may never know, rich with the romance of forgotten deeds no man can now trace, gone for ever like the smoke of last night's fire.

A lonely little lochan breaks into the roadway, its sole possessor, so far as I have ascertained, one trout, seemingly as proud of his domain as any Highland chieftain, and in his sudden leaps showing like a bar of rainbow.

Just here the railway—was ever railway so beautifully and unobtrusively situated—suddenly changes its position. One moment it forms a silent guard on the right, and as we dip under the bridge, almost as if by magic, it marches on our left.

In front the vista is now magnificent in its stretch and charm. Bare rock-strewn hills on the right, beautifully wooded slopes on the left, with the Dochart hurrying through the glen, the sun and some wonderful cloud effects above—and amidst it all a great silence.

Just above stands what you might well mistake for the falling ruins of a commonplace cottage, but it is one with a history attached, because at one time it was the home of Rob Roy.

Scramble up the bank and examine it and you will agree the site was well-chosen, indeed one more admirable for a man who might have to flee from his enemies at any moment would be hard to find. From here the glen is open for miles, and the giant bulk of Ben More affords shelter from the winds, protection against a sudden attack in that quarter, and a ready retreat in case of emergency. Behind, the hills are rock-strewn, and it would be difficult to track a nimble hardy man who knew every secret path and hidie-hole. At the very door lies a deep, bracken-clad gash in the hill-side, just the place for slinking off to cover unnoticed.

Here in the olden days a man might live his life free and unfettered, his every need supplied from the land at his door.

Low down by yon burn that's half-hidden in heather,
  He lurked like a lion in the lair he knew well ;
'Twas there sobbed the red-deer to feel his keen dagger,
  There pierced by his arrow the cailzie-cock fell.

Another enchanted mile or two and there, a few hundred yards from the roadway, stands what appears to be a solitary sheep-pen, guarded by an ancient tree. Something about it attracted, and on approaching I found it to be a burial-place of the MacNabs.

Here on this little knoll, quaint and silent amongst the hills, lie the kilted warriors of a bygone day—

the stones, those not under the moss of a century are too lichen-covered to be clearly decipherable. On a number of these old tombstones are carved queer, bearded faces, and I thought of the far-off times when the coronach would wail for the chiefs who are gone—unknown to-day to all but their direct descendants.

Opposite is Suie Lodge, and on making inquiries at the smiling, soft-tongued Highland woman in charge, she could give me no information, but suggested I might inquire at the hotel a little farther up the glen.

There, in Luib Hotel, with its golden eagle guarding the rods, baskets and waders, they told me something of its story and the prestige of the Clan MacNab.

Many are the tales told of the clan, and in truth this district more than holds its own in cruel deeds and relentless feuds.

Here is one incident of the less grim order told of the MacNab, who was prone occasionally to get into financial difficulties. One evening a sheriff-officer called to present a summons, but before he could perform his duties the laird invited him to enter his abode and partake of refreshment. Whisky was, of course, produced, and the officer was well plied with it, while, acting on instructions, some of the men hastily constructed an effigy and hung it upon a tree at a little distance from the fortress.

In the morning the man of law bethought him of his legal duties, but on glancing out of the window he was horrified to observe the dummy body swinging from a branch.

ROB ROY'S COTTAGE, GLENDOCHART

LOCH TAY FROM KILLIN

" What is that ? " he asked, falling into the trap so artfully prepared for his special benefit.

" It's nothing," replied his hearer ; " just a messenger of some kind who tried to force a summons on the laird."

The messenger-at-arms left for Edinburgh without undue delay, and took his summons back with him, having no wish to grace in turn the dule tree of a Highland gentleman !

While smiling and peaceful to-day, the glen can assume at certain seasons a wild and almost savage desolation. More than once have I seen the winding burn break its bounds and spread to the dimensions of a small loch, here or there a semi-submerged tree pointing the depth and overflow of the turbulent waters.

One old authority who explored the district in the last years of the eighteenth century tells of the rapid climatic changes to which Glendochart was subject. Sometimes the snow lay deep ; at other times the glen was swept by torrential rains. Severe frost held it in a vice-like grip—then suddenly and without warning came the thaw. Oftentimes huge avalanches of snow and rocks would come tumbling down the hill-sides, carrying everything in their path to ruin and destruction.

He relates how one evening night had hardly fallen, when one of these mighty snowfalls came tumbling down the hill-side. In its path lay a cottage, and the family were gathered round the peat-fire awaiting their evening meal. In a moment they were overwhelmed and buried beneath a mass of snow and rocks, everyone that is, except the mother, who was probably in another part of the cottage busy with her task.

But to-day there is no hint of storm or terror— every prospect is bright and fair.

St Fillan had associations with this district, and just hereabouts, where the roads diverge, was enacted a scene strange even in the annals of the Westland.

More than usual mystery surrounds the burial-place of St Fillan, even allowing for the lack of actual knowledge of what happened in the far-off seventh century, midway through which the Saint took farewell of the world.

When St Fillan died at Dundurn, the natives naturally desired his bones to rest in their midst, but there were other claimants. He was carried through Glenogle until the bodyguard arrived at this road-junction near Killin, and there a fierce altercation arose as to the direction in which the cortege should now proceed. Claymores were drawn and blows exchanged, so determined were the two factions to secure the honour of providing sepulture.

And then a miracle was performed. Where before one coffin had lain there were now two, and each party, reverently raising one, carried it off in opposite directions !

As the road gets narrower and more winding the great bulk of Ben Lawers, snow-capped and stark, becomes more dominant, dwarfing his neighbours.

Surely no town ever had more picturesque approach than this old-time Highland village of Killin. Guarded by a narrow bridge, on the left

the falls of Dochart, a wonderful series of broken
steps and, even this morning when anglers are
complaining of low waters, a sight to remember.

The Dochart here divides into two channels and
so creates a small, coffin-shaped island, hallowed
ground inasmuch as it forms the burying-place of
the MacNabs.

The approach is guarded by a locked gate, but
the keeper of the keys was not to be found, so
vaulting the dyke I easily gained admission by going
underneath the bridge and crossing the stream by
some large stones.

Here is peace. The ground deep in beech mast,
the sanctuary screened by trees—surely an ideal
place to rest until the great day when clan feuds
shall be forgotten and all tartans will rank alike.

There is one outstanding tree amongst the many
guarding those who sleep — a tall birch. Its
branches droop as if in mourning for its charges,
and sadness is depicted in every twig. It may seem
fanciful, but if ever tree spoke by outward sign
and symbol, this old birch mourns the clansmen it
has seen laid at its feet for generations past.

The name Killin means, according to some
authorities, the burial-place of Fingal, and as he
was a great Celtic warrior in his day, I went to
view his grave.

It stands on a brae-side midway through the
village, and to reach it one must pass a tradesman's
yard. Here I found a man busy painting a sign,
and to " pass the time of day " I asked him whose
grave that was in front.

" Rob Roy's, I think," said he !

The headstone has every appearance of great age, and undoubtedly the formation of the ground is reminiscent of a grave, but I believe the place was probed or examined many years ago and no urn or remains were discovered.

Still, let us preserve our traditions and beliefs, and for sentiment's sake I hope the great Prince of Morven, so immortalised by his son Ossian, is really resting there !

There is another monument here, also erected to a saint, but of much later date, one James Stewart, who flourished here as minister in the middle part of the eighteenth century. His life is notable for the fact that he translated the New Testament into Gaelic, and partly completed a like work on the Old, finished by his son, Dr Stewart, who was minister of Luss, on Loch Lomondside.

Alexander Campbell, whose " Journey from Edinburgh through Parts of North Britain " was published in 1802, has much sage advice and information to impart, and, like all who want to see the beauties of the land, he visited Killin. He has devoted considerable space to this place, even to quoting prices charged for provisions at the time of his visit, and tells us that beef, mutton, veal and pork averaged 3d. per lb. of 17½ oz. ; butter 9d. per lb. of 22 oz. ; and cheese from 5s. to 7s. per stone of 22 lbs.

But it is when he waxes eloquent about the people, their customs and feuds, that I like him best.

Here is a literal quotation, which is not un-interesting, and it will be observed I have not departed from his spelling. The italics, too, are as the author placed them :

"The *Macdonells* of Keappoch, a brave and resolute race of warriors, and the *Campbells* of Braidalbane, a numerous and no less warlike people, were continually making inroads on one another's lands. A desperate conflict took place on the hill rising immediately above the church of *Killin*, called *Stronachlachan*, undertaken by the brother of Keappoch, and a number of his followers, against the inhabitants of *Bunrannoch* and *Strathtay*.

"The *Macdonells*, who had travelled from their fastnesses in *Brae-lochaber*, over the mountains, through *Rannoch*, and Glenlion, had carried off all the cattle on their way southward ; and returning with their booty, by the heights of *Deiffer*, which run along the South side of *Loch-tay*, they had ascended *Stronachlachan* ; when tidings of their progress reached a party of *Campbells* who were assembled in the Hall of *Finlarig* at a christening.

" Fired with indignation at so daring an insult, they instantly rushed forth, ascended the hill, and attacked the foe, but were repulsed with loss.

"The *Macdonells*, triumphant, pursued their route ; but the Campbells receiving a reinforcement, as well they might on their own lands, followed the enemy, and came up with him on the braes of *Glenurcha*, where they overpowered him by numbers, recovered the booty, and returned in triumph, having accomplished their revenge."

This wild affray really arose, I believe, from the fact that the reivers (they were actually the Macdonalds of Glencoe) were attempting to drive

F

their booty across the Breadalbane lands without paying the customary " road collop."

This " road collop " was a certain percentage of the spoil due to another clan through whose territory a drove of " lifted " or stolen cattle was driven. In its time the custom gave rise to many wild occasions, indeed one notable example of its far-reaching possibilities was a battle-royal between the M'Intoshes and the Munros.

A party of the Munros were returning from Edinburgh to their homes in the far North.

They were mounted, for the journey was a long and tiresome one, and on their halting for the night somewhere in the Athole country, the owner of the land, when darkness fell, had the tails cut off their horses !

This was of course an unforgivable insult, but the Munros were not in sufficient strength to take immediate action, and so proceeded on their homeward journey.

Arriving at their chief stronghold, the Fiery Cross went round, and soon an eager band of armed men came south to pay their clansmen's debts ! And in full measure did they carry out their self-appointed task. Houses were given to the flames, no living soul who crossed their path was spared, and a great drove of cattle was carried off as spoil.

On passing through the M'Intosh lands the usual " road collop " was demanded.

Then followed some argument, summarily ended by Munro stating that he would give no more, and if the quota was not considered generous enough he would withdraw it altogether.

The M'Intoshes were not at strength and with drew, threatening to return and take all.

Munro knew they would honour their threats, and so ordering the least able of his following to drive the cattle straight across the hills for home, he and his fighting clansmen kept to the road, which passed not far from Inverness.

Soon the M'Intoshes were hot-foot on the wake of their enemies, and a desperate conflict ensued. M'Intosh and more than half of his clansmen were slain, but not without considerable loss to the Munro faction.

Never have I seen such a profusion of daffodils —only rivalled by the primroses which flourished everywhere—while the blackthorn formed a snowy mass of scented blossom.

No one can sojourn in Killin without visiting the ruins of Finlarig Castle, at one time a principal seat of the Breadalbane Campbells.

An avenue of ancient beech trees leads towards this old fortress, and time-worn as they are, they are guarded by the stumps of a former generation, planted, it is said, by one Donnacha Dubh a Churichie, or Black Duncan of the Cowl, a heartless warrior who for long occupied the place.

To gain admittance one rings a bell, suspended from the main gate, and supposed to be the nose of a shell used in the Egyptian war !

A quaint old stone sundial stands here, although now long past its duty days, a mere curio from the past. At one time I understand it not merely told the hour, but also gave the moon and tides.

It is said to be the only survivor of its kind in Scotland.

Scarcely less interesting is the fleur-de-lis carved on the guardian wall.

Indeed it is a warlike environment.

In front of the castle entrance is a pit, some six or seven feet deep, paved throughout and still furnished with two massive iron chains. On the edge is a stone with a hole in the centre, and captives whose birth or estate forbade hanging were allowed the honour of placing their heads on the stone, when the executioner soon relieved them of further worry in this world.

Inside the castle proper are a number of ancient stones and carvings, one particularly pointed out being that of a knight spanking his wife, so that the domestic hours in those old times were no less exciting than those spent on the field or in the chase !

The old gallows tree still flourishes notwithstanding its awful past, but the branch from which Black Duncan's victims made their exit from the world, and on which the mark of the rope was said to have been quite distinct, was blown down on the night of the Tay Bridge disaster. The trunk is now a mere shell, and some stormy night the ghosts of Black Duncan's victims will gather round it, and when the day breaks the locals will talk of how the wind seemed to shriek round the castle that night and the old gallows tree was blown down. Its stormy end, as I forecast it, will never occur to them, and they will never know how retribution came to Finlarig !

OLD STONE FIGURES IN FINLARIG CASTLE

If the invasion comes from the proper airt the great tree will lie prone at the foot of the justice knowe, surmounted as it is by the old holly tree under which Black Duncan sat and delivered his ruthless judgments of pit and gallows, and where justice was rarely tempered with mercy. It will be a mete end to its iniquitous old career.

The newer leaves of the venerable holly are prickly and fresh, but those on the aged branches are smooth and dull, bald with their burden of years.

Here every ben has given back again the echoes of the fierce clan slogans and the clash of steel, but as I turned my back on the ancient citadel and came down the steep narrow path, not even a bird broke the silent stillness, and only the century-old trees seemed to whisper in the shadows of the coming night.

> The shades of eve come slowly down,
> The woods are wrapped in deeper brown.

The beech leaves of last summer rustled on the path, the old giving place to the new; an owl screeched from somewhere in the gathering darkness—and then a light glinted through the trees, and I knew the hotel was just across the wooden bridge.

VI

PONTIUS PILATE'S BIRTHPLACE

There's naething but the sheep tae see—or deer upon the hill,
The cloud-scarves waivin' roun' the ben—the liltin' o' a rill;
Just miles o' purple heather—an' the bracken on the brae,
But it's a' that I wad ask for in the langest day.

It is, I think, admitted that Pontius Pilate probably first saw the stars in Britain, and as tradition has settled on Fortingall as his birthplace, for the glamour of the thing I am taking it for granted. After all is said and done, it is quite likely, and many claims are nowadays projected which rest on more gossamer foundations.

Be that as it may, to-day my road led by the winding side of Loch Tay, but at the moment the Lochay was my companion, and its garrulous chatter was counter-balanced by the silent heather-clad braes on the left.

Black Duncan of the Cowl was patron of this district, and ruled and rustled it with the best. Patron he may have been—but saint he certainly was not.

One thing I will say for him—land-grabbing Campbell as he was—his heritage of trees (for he was a master arboriculturist) was his good deed in his day.

That he was a true friend I doubt, but there were no two minds about his hatreds. A lovelace, he was survived by some thirty children, and combined with his feuds and forays the skill of a scheming statesman and the light gift of the poetaster.

As has already been told, he used to sit in judgment under his ancient holly, sending his captives to the right or left as seemed best in his sage opinion. His edicts would probably be carried out on the instant, so that, on one hand, his victims would adorn the old oak tree while, on the other, the blade would drink deep in the pit. Doubtless he would gloat over the untimely end of many a brave fellow whose tartan was for the time in ill-favour with the lord of Finlarig and his nefarious plots and schemes.

To-day such scenes are far down the avenue of history, and the charming tree-lined roadway is peaceful enough in the moist August sunshine.

For the moment mighty Ben Lawers with his attendant Beinn Ghlas, which for the past hour have dominated the view, are hidden by the verdure.

The rowans are plentiful : yellow where they fight for precedence with their strong growing competitors ; scarlet where the sun has touched them, but always charming to the eye.

Loch Tay, which for the past mile or two had hidden amongst her sentinel trees, now came dramatically into the open.

Larch, chestnut, oak, ash, silver fir and the fruitful rowan make the way gay and beautiful, till once again the loch sinks behind the host of trees and hides for a little as if conscious of the wealth of charm she has to contend against, only once more to appear in a long silver streak, more reminiscent of a wide embracing river than a Highland loch.

Trees are always graceful things, but I cannot remember any season when they looked so radiantly beautiful, due perhaps to the heavy rains. Indeed, this summer has produced a garniture of flower and berry, rich in fragrant colouring, which has made the field and hedgeway, moor and woodland, a special joy and pleasure.

Loch Tay must be traversed twice, once either way, ere it can be appreciated, even by the casual passer-by; but so much is secret, hidden by the woods and hills, that only a lifetime's acquaintance will enable you to understand.

But all is dwarfed by Lawers, a great rambling hulk of a mountain, which looks even mightier and more majestic at a distance.

On the farther shore the towering hills are tree-clad at the base, giving way to a purple stretch and shading off to a brilliant green again at the higher altitudes.

So land-locked does the loch appear here that for a little I lost it completely; nothing on either side but sloping braes, thick in sturdy bracken, with the bold and irrepressible peak of Tullich crowning all.

Round the bend, and once more the full stretch of the loch, now carrying a slight mist which adds to, rather than detracts from, its charm.

Ben Lawers now towers above us, an easy hill to climb and a paradise for the botanist.

There is a tale that at one time the men of this

district were veritable Samsons for strength. When engaged on military duty, strict orders were given that no man was to pass a certain milestone, under severe penalty. Now it so happened—and perhaps that may have been the reason for this restriction—that the inn was situated some little distance on the wrong side of the boundary. Anxious to enjoy its forbidden delights, and yet afraid openly to break bounds, one of the men, big John, carried the milestone with him—and so kept within his orders !

Shortly after we pass the Ben there opens up the most beautiful vista of all. The road starts to wind slowly downhill, the loch opens out—the right arm stretching as far as one can see until it merges in the vision with the dark woods which appear to stand knee-deep in the water ; the immediate foreground a range of huge bens, green, purple and black as the sun kindles them, sombre and awe-inspiring.

Mark the spot, because here you will find something of interest. The roadway is bordered by a moss-clad stone dyke, and in the field above stands a noble tree, easily distinguished by its bifurcated trunk. Almost under its spreading branches you will find a stone, older probably than its guardian. It is an interesting relic, and the inscription runs :

TRADITION SAYS THIS STONE
IS THE FAIR OR MARKET
CROSS OF FERNAN.
AND THE LEGEND IS
" CURSED BE HE WHO REMOVES IT "
BREADALBANE.

The panorama is now a changing prospect of loch, wood and hill, almost every step producing a new and varying picture.

Here I parted company with the loch and took the narrow road for Fortingall, and almost at once a token of bygone days meets the eye. Under a plane tree, open and unprotected save by the goodwill of the passer-by, stands an old stone baptismal font, brimming to-day with soft rain-water from the Glenlyon hills.

It is all that now remains to mark the spot where in other generations stood a church dedicated to Saint Ciaran.

The river which runs alongside is the Lyon, dashing its crystal amber waters into foam in its anxiety to join the loch, while around, the hills seem to crowd suddenly together, adding a black sombreness to the scene.

On the left is the forbidding entrance to Glen-lyon, once a Clan Gregor stronghold, but lost by that tragic clan in the old turbulent days of the past.

> Glenorchy's proud mountains, Kilchurn and her towers,
> Glenstrae and Glenlyon no longer are ours,
>   We're landless, landless, landless.

Sometimes of a winter's evening, when thinking of the lonely hills and glens, my mind dwells for a space on dark Glenlyon, and I wonder if any poor mortal is groping his way along its stygian paths. In summer, one of the most winsome roads I know, but with a sudden trick of changing to an awesome dreary way when the mists gather and the sun hides. Below the roadway the dark turgid stream ;

on either hand trees in abundance, while towering above are the purple hills.

To walk alone through Glenlyon in the gloaming, rain and mist competing, never a living soul to hail, is only in small measure to realise the trials and miseries of a broken man in the days when the strong arm alone ruled. It is impossible to appreciate fully what life meant in those times, but whatever wrongs were committed when greed and secret council went hand in hand, to me Glenlyon seems a stage to suit the tragic stories of the past more fittingly than most.

Never can I forget one September evening traversing the glen which beckons to one at Bridge of Balgie, some miles up Glenlyon, and joins the main road again where the little church looks down on Loch Tay.

What a wondrous glen-road it is ! Its startling beauty is almost unreal, so haunting is its charm.

Picture a huge cleft amongst the hills, shaped like the letter V. From top to base on either side a thick quilt of purple heather, the narrow track, clinging and winding for miles in front, the only break in the hill-side. Below, a brawling stream, every foot white and foam-tormented, for all the world like a long tortuous waterfall. No other feature intervenes until a lonely mountain loch appears. Rarely is the silence violated by so much as a bird. Beautiful—grand—no words of mine can paint or do it justice. Sit for an hour and smoke—for you are away from the world, immured completely, alone with the hills.

If fate places you amongst her favoured ones and

you visit this glen of peace and silence, go afoot, for the road is like some you may know amongst the Galloway hills, too narrow for vehicles to pass in safety—a land made only for those who wish sanctuary and peace.

But that by-way has led away from Glenlyon and the task in hand ; still, who would grudge or mar the pleasure of mentally re-treading the old roads of yesterday—roads that come back unbidden to the mind at times with a keener zest and a greater joy than was to be obtained even in the actual tramping of them !

It is on the borders of two hundred years since Pennant adventured through Scotland and wrote his interesting account of the country and its characteristics.

He visited Glenlyon, on horseback I feel sure, and refers to a great clan battle which took place here between the MacKays and the MacGregors, and so fierce and bloody was the conflict that the waters were darkened with blood when the victors washed their weapons.

Another authority tells of a " great battle " which also found its stage in this glen, the contestants on this occasion being the notorious Wolf of Badenoch and the Clan MacIvor, and yet again the river was stained with the blood of the slain.

Campbells, Stewarts, Camerons, Athole men, to name only a few of the fierce brotherhoods, have in turn tried issue here.

And before their day, the great Fingall, renowned as a warrior, had twelve castles in the glen, or at

FORTINGAL—PONTIUS PILATE'S BIRTHPLACE

IN GLENOGLE

least so the tale goes, and perhaps that may have been the reason for its original name of Cromghleann-nan-clach or the Crooked Glen of the Stones, but that I cannot say.

But now the thatched roofs of Fortingall peep amongst the trees and the little old-world clachan draws near.

Right away sinister memories are awakened by the sight of Glenlyon House, which guards the approach to the village. For this was the home of Campbell, the man who carried through the blackest deed in Scottish history; from here he went to eat bread which could be ill-spared, to feign friendship with his hosts—and cut their throats by way of thanks. Aye, Glencoe was a bad blot on the page of Scottish history, and the terror of that night in the Glen o' Weeping is never likely to be effaced so long as heather grows or tales are told. A black business indeed.

> Leave the blood upon his bosom,
>   Wash not off that sacred stain ;
> Let it stiffen on the tartan,
>   Let his wounds unclosed remain,
> Till the day when he shall show them,
>   At the throne of God on high,
> When the murderers and the murdered,
>   Meet before the Judge's eye !

Charles II is supposed to have said " there never was a rebellion in Scotland without either a Campbell or a Dalrymple at the bottom of it," but this was far worse than an open rebellion. Only, perhaps, after the '45 was such calculating, heartless cruelty again conceived, and even Cumberland, bad as he was, might have stopped short at such nameless treachery. As Campbell himself admitted on one awful occasion, the curse of Glencoe followed him through the years. Some considerable time after the Glencoe horror, he was present at a military execution. A reprieve had arrived for the poor fellow under sentence, and when Campbell was drawing it from his pocket, his handkerchief dropped to the ground. This was the prearranged signal for the firing-party, and so the man was shot ere Campbell was aware of his mischance !

Fortingall, as we know it to-day, owes much to the late Sir Donald Currie. If neat, trim houses be the standard, then that model landowner did much to be thanked for. Personally, I like to see the typical crofter's home, with its low doorway and thatched roof, but I suppose comfort and a higher standard of living must come before pictur-esque effect, even in a Highland clachan !

For a place so steeped in tale and tradition, Fortingall has an unassuming exterior.

But if you saw in it just an attractive little village, a place in which to loiter for an hour and then pass on, you would be wrong.

There are several points of interest here, not least to me the old yew tree, probably the arborial veteran of Europe.

Go in by the gate which guards the little kirkyard, pass the model church, and there you will find this ancient yew, caged behind stone and railing to protect it from the thoughtless.

At one time it was wholly surrounded by masonry, but careful observers noted signs that such confinement was having an evil effect on the veteran, and so part of the wall was taken away and iron railings, admitting light and air, substituted.

Such a souvenir of other days wants careful nursing, and when its time comes to wither and die, the very hills will feel that they have lost a companion of their youth. I peered through the railing and examined it from every angle, because here was age in stark reality, a living thing which had braved life for two thousand five hundred years, indeed that may underestimate its age.

It would be a full-grown, matured citizen of the forest world some six or seven hundred years before Pontius Pilate was born, and yet here it is, green and fresh, a link with days so distant that we have lost their record !

No wonder its heart looks bad, its trunk here and there a mere shell, and that its back is slightly bent in part ; the burden of two thousand five hundred years is a heavy load to carry.

Pennant, already referred to, mentions the old yew tree, and gives its measurements as " fifty-six feet and a half in circumference."

But he gives other interesting figures which throw an illuminating light on the intervening years. On one side of Loch Tay, " within a radius of fifteen square miles, there lived seventeen hundred and eighty-six souls ; on the other side, almost twelve hundred."

The road which winds round the opposite side of the loch is one of the most beautiful by-passes in Scotland. It is, or should be, a preserve for the man with the haversack however ; at least it is not a good road for cars, and fortunately no provision is allowed for buses, and so it remains secluded and picturesque, a haven for the lover of beautiful paths and lovely trees, where walking is still a real pleasure, undisturbed and free.

Studded with ruined cottages—perhaps the one-time homes of the families Pennant speaks of—laced with rushing cascades, hazel patches and wild flowers in profusion, at every season a rambler's joy, no wonder it is a favourite land for brush and palette. More than once I have been astonished at the abnormal size of the hips—or fruit of the wild rose —hereabouts, and indeed in the autumn season they form a distinctive colour feature with their bright crimson and scarlet splashes against the fern banks.

Last time I passed that way, and a heartening walk it is, I was entertained by the sight of a model rock-garden adorning one of those ideal little residences which so often surprise one in out-of-the-way spots, and to observe two fat porkers rooting about amongst the plants !

No human soul was in evidence, and the magic of hill and loch threw a spell over the scene. To my mind the real charm of Loch Tay is only fully appreciated from this winding narrow pathway.

They were an industrious people on Lochtayside in Pennant's day, and when tending their cattle on the hill-sides they took their spinning-wheels with them and annually sold some fifteen hundred pounds worth of yarn at Taymouth fair.

But Taymouth, too, has lost its old-time glory. The home of the Breadalbanes is now a modern hotel, and golfers in plus-fours smoke cigarettes and discuss the merits of steel shafts underneath the crests and arms of men who played with sterner weapons.

The Breadalbane family name is Campbell, and the founder of the line arrived here somewhere about the end of the sixteenth century—Sir Colin of that ilk.

This gentleman, when it was pointed out to him that his house, instead of being in the centre of his land, had been erected at the eastern extremity, explained that he hoped to make the site the centre in due course, but his pious intentions were frustrated.

Chambers tells a good story of a Breadalbane who flourished many years ago.

When in London this young Earl fell in love with a daughter of the Earl of Holland. The young lady possessed in her own right a fortune of ten thousand pounds, and was the richest prize in the matrimonial market of her day.

His suit prospered, and soon the happy couple were wed.

After the ceremony, Breadalbane brought his young bride home to the ancestral hall—and the manner of their journey was strange, even for that day.

The Earl mounted his Highland sheltie, while his bride climbed up behind; on the other of his two ponies he had the ten-thousand-pound dowry in gold, guarded by their retainers, and so they made their strange, intriguing journey to the North!

But all that is beside the point and takes me away

G

for the moment from the old yew tree and the task in hand.

Another ancient tree grows close by, a chestnut, laden with "burs" enough to delight half the school lads in the parish. But old and mellow, as we reckon time, it is a stripling as the old yew counts the years, and its gently swaying branches are the mere exuberance of youth as compared with the stiff rustling of the ancient one.

At the church door stands what to me has the appearance of an old baptismal font; doubtless it too has witnessed many a strange affair in its day, weather worn with its weight of years.

In a field immediately opposite the hotel is to be seen a green mound, surmounted by a stone.

It is a grave, a community burial-place, with its rather gruesome story of a strong-minded heroine.

In the dark days of the plague Fortingall was no more fortunate than many other places. Death was abroad, and found many victims in this out-of-the-way Highland clachan. So rife was it that soon the dead outnumbered the living, and one old woman, carrying on with indomitable spirit brought the victims to this green spot and day by day added to the hecatomb. It is said she placed them on horseback—a patient old white horse—or dragged them on a rough sledge, and so was enabled to perform her self-appointed duty to her fellow villagers.

It took one of strong character to act her part and terrible as was the load fate placed on her shoulders, faith must have filled her heart and attuned her mind and will to her ghastly heritage.

That is the story as tradition hands it down, but later I was told a strange tale by one who is dowered with second sight.

My informant was passing Fortingall one bright sunny day and saw walking in the field beside the stone twelve nuns. They were dressed in garments composed of some rough cloth, but otherwise their habits were much the same as at the present time.

They appeared so natural that this gentleman supposed they were nuns staying in the village for a holiday or rest.

On his glancing at the other side of the road for an instant and looking towards the field again, the nuns had disappeared. By looking away he had lost the correct focus.

He got the impression that the stone marked their burial-place, and that they had lost their lives while nursing the villagers during the Black Plague. That impression was given to him by some outside influence which he could not describe or account for.

That indeed was not his only occult experience in this district. Last summer, accompanied by his wife, he was walking from Killin to Bridge of Lochy. They were walking by the road which leads up the left side of the Lochy. It was a bright summer day, without a shadow or cloud in the sky.

On his passing a mound of stones in the field just before reaching the farm, something there attracted his attention.

My friend's wife suddenly said : " Don't you see figures of men sitting on these stones ? "

" Yes," answered my friend; " there are quite a

number of them : they all wear the kilt, and their leader has on a steel helmet."

His wife also noted these facts, and apparently conscious that they were observed, the leader came to his feet and gave the salute.

My friend informed me that many years ago a fierce clan battle was fought on the spot and that the stones cover the burial-place of the dead, who, according to him, are for some reason earth-bound.

To me the second sight is an uncanny thing, but be that as it may, later, as I stood at the hotel window and again saw the green mound in its lonely field, but now in the gathering darkness and under a drenching rain, I could scarce forbear a shudder as I turned towards the glowing peat-fire.

VII

THROUGH GLENOGLE
TO BALQUHIDDER

Long before the towns were built,
　　Far behind the years,
Came the Roman cohorts in their pride.
　　Here the kilted clansmen,
　　And the hardy lowland spears,
Fought their way to freedom e'er they died.

SOME weeks, months almost, were to pass ere I was on the open road again.

Spring, with her promise, was over. Summer, heavy with fulfilment, was gradually losing her ornate tints, and the wind this morning had a bite, early in August as it was.

The dog roses, which had rioted in such profusion of pink and white, no longer made the hedgerows gay with colour, while their compensating heritage of hips still lacked the crimson polish. Like the fruit of the hawthorn—haws beloved in boyhood days—they hung in dull brown clusters— a mere promise of beauty to come when the last lingering hedgerow blossom had disappeared.

Gone, too, were the primroses and daffodils where before their yellow carpet, flanked by flaming whin and more delicate broom, had been a delight to the eye.

Lowliest of lovely things are they,
On earth that soonest pass away.

But Nature had merely changed her colour scheme, and to-day the foxglove flaunted her banners beneath the scented honeysuckle while the air was heavy with the perfume of queen-of-the-meadow.

In my own garden, ere I left, the Michaelmas daisies were on the point of bloom, a sure harbinger, in this district at least, that autumn tints of crimson, russet and gold would early displace the more delicate bounty of the wayside flowers.

The changing season brought one new glory—the heather was rioting over every hill-side, forming a purple garment which boded ill for the old cock grouse that nodded so complacently to me as I passed.

Poor old cock grouse—little did he wot that the sheep I met on the roadside a mile or two back were being moved to make his slaughter more certain.

It is necessary to retrace one's footsteps for a mile or two before leaving Killin and to pass once again Inchbhuidh, where the MacNabs sleep so soundly.

As the wild MacGregors were to the Colquhouns, so stood the MacNabs of other days to the Clan Neish.

The Clan MacNab, probably no worse than their neighbours in the old times, had certainly no monopoly of the virtues. One incident in their records can take its place with most.

For many years the MacNabs and the Neishes were at active and bitter feud. Long were they opposed, and open or covert acts of aggression and hatred seemed to keep the ill-blood at fever-heat.

On this memorable occasion they met openly in battle array and fought with such bitter ferocity that when the day was done only a remnant of the Neishes was left alive.

These men, about a dozen in number, sought refuge on an island in Loch Earn, acting under command of an old Highlander, a blood relative of their slain chieftain.

They lived by ravage and plunder, and as they possessed the only boat on the loch, their position was thought to be safe from all comers.

The MacNab chief of those days was a vindictive, unscrupulous old savage who could not stand to be crossed or contradicted, and whose rule was brutal and absolute.

One day a servitor, having been dispatched by MacNab to Crieff to purchase provisions for the Christmas festivities, was met and robbed by the Neishes; was indeed fortunate that his life was spared.

When the ghillie returned from his fruitless errand to the rocky stronghold of the MacNabs, the old man went almost demented with rage and venom, and brooded on his wrongs until, the day of the feast arriving, viewing his own scanty board, and thinking of his blood enemies carousing at his expense, he could contain himself no longer.

Turning to his twelve stalwart sons, he said, " the night is the night if the lads are the lads," a hint which required no stronger expression !

The twelve instantly got ready for their task,

and fully armed with pistol, dirk and claymore, they sallied forth to do their father's bidding and revenge their wrongs.

Knowing that without a boat their mission would prove a fruitless one, led by Smooth John, so called in irony because of his rough manner, they mounted their own boat on their shoulders and so carried it from Loch Tay to Loch Earn over mountain and burn, a seemingly impossible task. As a matter of fact, were it not vouched for, the undertaking seems beyond human endurance, but hatred of their enemies and an unholy enthusiasm gave them super-human endurance.

Never do I visit this region but that night's work comes uppermost in my thoughts. What men these brothers must have been. Strong, brawny, determined; feral and remorseless as the weasel which crossed their path—also engaged on its blood-thirsty expedition, but if anything on a higher moral plane, because it followed blind instinct in its blood-lust, not revenge and rapine.

Arriving at Loch Earn, they launched their boat and craftily approached the island, where the Neishes resided in a low-roofed hut.

But silence was unnecessary. With the exception of the ancient leader their enemies were in an intoxicated stupor, contributed alike by the MacNab plunder and their sense of security.

Bursting open the door, Smooth John and his brothers soon made short work of their hereditary foes.

Seizing the old leader by his white hair, John twisted his head and severed it with his claymore, while his brothers slaughtered the sleeping clansmen. Only a little boy escaped, by hiding near-by.

On their return, the MacNabs resolved to carry back their boat, but becoming fatigued—and little wonder—they dropped it on the hill-side, where it lay for many years, until in time it rotted and disappeared.

They took the severed head of old Neish with them and presented it to their stern old sire, who called for whisky, and, it is stated, in common with his warrior sons, got drunk with joy!

From what I have gleaned, the MacNabs of bygone days were a fiery, quick-tempered race who brooked no interference with their rights and privileges—real or fancied.

A story goes that on one occasion a laird of MacNab, with a company of what were then known as the Breadalbane Fencibles, was proceeding from the West to Dunfermline, and in addition to their lawful baggage there was concealed a considerable quantity of whisky! Some spy or traitor had given away the secret, and when the Fencibles were somewhere in the vicinity of Alloa, a party of excisemen that had been lying in wait came forward to appropriate the smuggled whisky. MacNab, as a chief who placed a high value on his personal position, was marching in a stately manner some little distance in advance of his party, when one of the men hurriedly approached and informed him what was toward.

" Did the lousy villains *dare* to obstruct the march of the Breadalbane Highlanders ? " he shouted, and immediately hurried to the scene of operations.

Asking the officials, in none too polite terms, who they were and what they wanted, he was told by their spokesman, " gentlemen of the excise."

" Robbers and thieves, you mean," shouted the enraged MacNab, and insisted on the production of their commissions.

Not expecting any such contretemps, they had not considered it necessary to bring documentary evidence of their status.

" Just what I thought," roared the laird; " a parcel of highway robbers and thieves." And turning to the baggage party he shouted, " Prime ! load ! " but the excisemen did not await the third order, and made for Alloa at top speed.

" Now, my lads," said the laird, " proceed—your whisky's safe."

But to the road. To pass under the railway bridge is like opening the door of another room. The setting at once changes, and the green hills guarding Glenogle stand arrayed on every side. The roadside was garlanded with bloom. King's-bedstraw, harebells, foxgloves, meadow-sweet, and a profusion of our own hardy, dauntless Scotch thistle.

What a defiant-looking plant this same old thistle is, almost conscious of its dignity as the national emblem. But the burden seems to weigh lightly on its rugged head, and its " touch-me-gin-ye-daur " attitude is alike uncompromising for Scot or foreigner, friend or foe.

I stopped to admire one particularly splendid

specimen carrying aloft its many purple crowns, and thought of the noble work its progenitors did so many centuries ago, so that to-day it is looked up to by every true native as his guerdon and exemplar. It has a lesson for most of us, this rugged old flower.

Its sturdy independence, thrawn purple-faced old Scot as it is, makes it worthy of Maclagan's verse :

> Hurrah for the thistle, the bonnie Scotch thistle !
> The evergreen thistle of Scotland for me.
> Awa' wi the flowers in your lady-built bowers,
> The strong-bearded, weel-guarded thistle for me !

In any case there are no lady-built bowers here-abouts ; indeed Glenogle is one of the wildest spots I know. At one part in particular, so studded it is with huge rough boulders that I sometimes wonder how the avalanche which seems so imminent does not sweep down the mountain-side and carry the railway line to chaos in the burn below.

The Scottish Kyber Pass, Queen Victoria is reputed to have aptly named it.

The road got wilder as it ascended, with a fine white-flecked, peaty-looking burn brawling along on the right.

The day had promised rain since early morning, and just as I passed Lairig Cheile, nestling alone here by the roadside, down it came.

No gentle smirr, but a very deluge. Mist suddenly enveloped the hills, and on the other side of the glen, in the distance, it seemed to drift along like huge clouds of steam.

But where I was it was no picturesque drift; rain evidently meant to do its worst, and in a few minutes white foaming torrents were rushing down the hill-sides, turning almost cream-colour in their rage. Rarely have I seen such heavy rain, and the mist on the hill-tops made the scene dark and wild. There was no thunder, unfortunately, to add solemnity to the setting, which became more desolate the higher I mounted.

In half an hour, after everything, myself included, was saturated and in a thoroughly miserable condition, the mists rolled away, the sun smiled, and disclosed the rows of hills and bens towards which lay my goal.

The sun was shining again, but Loch Earn was carrying white horses as I passed. Unfortunately my road to-day led away from the loch-side, and a beautiful vista of tree-spanned, troubled water was my only reward.

The bare hill-sides now gave place to roadside trees and wooded slopes, where on the left lies Ardvorlich, now home of the Stewarts.

There was little traffic; indeed the place seemed deserted until one hurrying motorist arrived and caused commotion enough during his momentary passing; indeed never until to-day did I know that a hen had so many feathers.

Quietly walking along the highway, which at this point is straight and level, I saw a sedate-looking white hen on the roadside. A car, coming at speed, appeared at the bend, and just then the hen, in that wayward manner germane to the species, took thought to cross the road. Part running, part flying in a heavy manner, it was too slow for fate, and the oncoming car caught it on the radiator. The impact was quite audible, and of a sudden the camber was white with feathers, for all the world as if someone had emptied a bolster.

Of the hen I had seen my last, and it was being borne towards the city on the bonnet or wings of the car.

After one passes Balquhidder station the view is as perfect as I can imagine. Green hills, richly wooded at the base, tall bracken, and guarded in the distance by blue-black mountains, rugged and stern. Every change of light or shade varies the scene, but morning, high noon, or evening, it is to me a wonderful picture.

A mile or two of this rapture-compelling scenery, and then Kingshouse. Here I left the main highway and took the by-pass towards Balquhidder. In front lie the Braes o' Balquhidder, sung so sweetly by Tannahill :

> Now the summer's in prime,
>   Wi' the flowers richly blooming,
> And the wild mountain thyme,
>   A' the moorlands perfuming.

The whole place seemed deserted, void of human activity, when quite unexpectedly I came upon a beautiful little church. Surrounded by a high wall, with trees growing it seemed to the very door, so small that it appeared almost as if some architect had made a model for a beautiful cathedral—for a cathedral in miniature it verily looked—and left it here to be called for. The wall was too high to scale, the huge iron gates were securely locked, and so I had to content myself with gazing longingly through the bars. What a difficult thing it is to gain access to a Scottish church unless a service is in progress! No church door stands invitingly open to anyone who wants to worship quietly alone. Always you must be one of a crowd, with an organist perfunctorily stumbling through the ill-chosen music. Tired nerves—heavy hearts—find little peace in such surroundings, and the sanctuary of a quiet pew for undisturbed meditation is ill to find.

An old farmer—a genial soul—who passed, informed me that if it was Rob Roy's grave I sought, the kirkyard where he lay was about a mile or so farther on.

He spoke with that charming West Highland accent, and was so obviously anxious to be helpful, that thanking him for his courtesy, I walked towards the MacGregor's last resting-place.

In the shadow of an old ruined church, looking down on Loch Voil, the redoubtable outlaw shares his grave with Mary, his wife, and two of their five sons, Coll and Robert.

The wind for his watcher, the mist for his shroud,
  Where the green and the grey moss will weave their
    wild tartans,
A covering meet for a chieftain so proud.

This is a land with a battle history, where pride and passion held sway and no man craved stronger passport than his own right arm.

MacLarens, MacGregors, Buchanans, Grahams, Stewarts—all have played a part here. Each clan has taken its share in turning the beautiful, smiling country-side into a cockpit, and many a squabble— frequently open conflict—has been enacted in view of the hoary old kirk.

> Often, alas, the fiery cross was sped,
>   And hills resounded the wild battle-cry ;
> Wars of extermination fierce were waged,
>   Most dreadful in their wanton cruelty.

Balquhidder, although so intimately associated with Rob Roy and his family, is Clan MacLaren country.

Not far from this spot took place one of those savage clan battles so often arising out of mere trifles, magnified by the uncompromising clan feeling and native pride.

This affair was no exception, and seen through modern eyes it appears to be a mere trial of savage strength and prowess.

The apparent cause of this bloody conflict appears almost childish to one who digs no deeper than the obvious facts. Clan feeling, of course, explains much, and the wrongs of other days were the basic reason for much that is obscure.

Before the coming of modern Poor Laws almost every village had its " natural," who, because of his affliction, was given more liberty of deed and speech than would be tolerated from a more normal character. Most middle-aged people will recollect the type who, in our less tolerant age, have disappeared from public life. Consanguinity was, perhaps, the root cause for much, but be that as it may, every village had its " Heather Jock " or some such creature ; taken for granted in most cases, occasionally almost public characters. Remember it was the disappearance of Daft Jamie which led to the discovery of the grisly doings of Burke and Hare in a city so large as Edinburgh. Think what the molestation of a mental case would mean if the aggressor was a member of another clan where in any case little love was lost betwixt the tartans.

Here, then, was the stage set and ready.

One of the MacLarens of Balquhidder was of the above type. Attending the annual fair of St Kessaig, held at Kilmahog, not far from Callander, one of the Buchanans of Leny, in passing, knocked off MacLaren's bonnet with a salmon he happened to be carrying. MacLaren told him he would not dare to repeat the act at next St George's fair, held in Balquhidder, and the matter apparently ended there. When the Balquhidder fair came round the Buchanans attended in force, fully armed and determined to prove their strength and daring.

Then, for the first time, the insulted MacLaren told his friends how he had been treated at Kilmahog. At once the Fiery Cross was sent round, and every able-bodied MacLaren hastened to obey.

The rage and impatience of the insulted clansmen was such that they impetuously attacked the Buchanans ere their muster was complete or their forces in order. As a result they were driven from the field in disorder. Victory seemed to lie with the Buchanans until a MacLaren clansman, observing his son being cut down by an opponent, caught the " madness of battle," and shouting the war-cry of his clan, rushed again to the attack. The MacLarens rallied, advanced once more upon their seemingly victorious enemy, and by sheer desperation carried the day. Only two Buchanans escaped from the carnage, later to be slain by their implacable clan foes.

The MacLaren were an old clan and a proud, and many and deadly were their feuds with neighbouring septs. But they went even further than most, insomuch that no man was allowed to enter the Balquhidder church on Sabbath until the last MacLaren was seated !

Naturally, this attitude was bitterly resented by those of a different name, and many fierce quarrels and scuffles took place at the church door.

To-day all names are alike in value, and in the little modern church no man has a prescriptive right in his worship.

The afternoon was waning as I left the old kirkyard, but I decided there was still time to traverse the loch-side to Inverlochlarig and see the house where Rob Roy died.

Narrow the road is, too restricted for the modern speed merchant, and fairly embowered in trees.

I had not gone more than a few yards when a something, which at first glance I mistook for a brown and withered fern, suddenly came to life, scampered along the bank and shot up a tree, so incredibly quick were its movements. A squirrel it was, not the lazy pampered animal of the South, but a denizen of the wild, quick as a flash in its

H

movements and immersed in pre-winter arrangements.

The road wound on in its undisturbed beauty, sloping braes on the right, on the left the loch. No sign of man and his handiwork unless a huge square mound of cut bracken in an open space amongst the trees, the work of someone preparing bedding against the time when winter's snows demanded a warm byre for his bestial.

After I passed Craigruie House, silent and deserted amongst the trees, the character of the scenery gradually changed.

Sunshine, greenery and the bloom of wild flowers gave place to a stage amongst the most rugged and lonely of the West.

Bog-myrtle and ferns in profusion, wet peaty soil, a long strath hemmed round by towering bens. The mist came down again, creeping almost to the loch-side, sheets of rain swept across the water, and a more desolate, lonely spot I have not yet traversed. Not so much as a water-hen amongst the reeds ; no wailing cry of peesweep or whaup ; just rain, mist and silence.

On the left I caught a glimpse of a square stone wall enclosing a few yards of hill-side, almost enveloped by an old rowan tree.

Surmising its purpose I scrambled through the peat bog—for it was little more—and sure enough it was an old-time burial-place. The iron gate was locked, but the wall had fallen in at one part, and soon I stood amongst the long wet grass.

Only one stone was visible, old and weather-beaten, the arms at the head undecipherable. So far as I could make out, the last tenant died in 1744. Under the overflowing branches of the rowan borne down with the weight of unripe green berries was another stone, but so draped in the moss of years that its message to the living must have disappeared several generations ago.

I squelched back again through the bog and peat to the narrow roadway, but by now the spectral mist had shrouded even the near-by hills and the place was lonely and silence-stricken.

The hard road surface (and it was surprisingly good) gave place to a muddy path which at once led to a fast-flowing brown stream. Farm-carts cross here by a ford, too deep to-day for safety, but a swinging wooden bridge took charge of pedestrians.

And so I reached the house where Rob Roy died. Not facing his foes, claymore in hand as would appear a suitable end for such as he, but in his bed like any peaceful dweller in the glen.

When Rob Roy was on his death-bed, indeed in his last hours, he was told that one of his enemies wished to visit him, and was indeed without.

"Raise me from my bed," was his response, "throw me my plaid around me, and bring me my claymore, dirk and pistols—it shall never be said that a foeman saw Rob Roy MacGregor defenceless and unarmed."

Implacable to the last, during the brief interview, we are told, he maintained a "cold and haughty civility," and when his one-time enemy left he ordered the pipes to play "ha til mi tulidh," and expired before the dirge was finished. So passed a figure to live in memory as long as tales of strife and daring hold hearts in thrall—an outlaw, but like Robin Hood, a friend of the poor.

> They were suited well to their own rude times,
>   And ours will not let them go,
> Till the last of Scotland's sons shall say—
>   'Mid the final wrecks below—
>   " Ha til, ha til me tulidh ! "

To-day, of course, hardly any part of the original house remains. It is inhabited by some half-dozen shepherds, who live their lonely lives remote on the hill-sides.

A woman from the modern farm-house adjacent looks after their meals, but she was no historian. She had heard of Rob Roy, but he was before her time, and so was only of passing interest. " The men knew," she said ; but the men were not about, and the day was rapidly giving place to evening.

From here a good hill-man would find it not too difficult to make over the hills to Crianlarich, Ardlui or Stronachlachar, as he thought best. They are almost equidistant and are really not far as miles go, although some good hills intervene.

Every crag, every mountain-side hereabouts must have been familiar ground to Rob Roy. Isolated, free from the harrying blades of his enemies, well-nigh an inviolable sanctuary. If his eager spirit and sense of oppression had been less dominant he might have lived a happier life—who knows—but even so, Scotland had lost a page of her romance, the glamour of which shall last as long as his native hills and glens.

IN GLENOGLE—NOTE THE THREE BRIDGES—ON LEFT, SAID TO BE THE ROMAN ROAD ; CENTRE, GENERAL WADE'S ROAD ; AND ON RIGHT, MODERN HIGHWAY

For, free as the eagle, these rocks were his eyrie,
  And free as the eagle, his spirit shall soar.

But by now it was more than grey in the glen,
indeed darkness did not seem far away, and so I
turned for home by the way I had come, nine long
hill-miles towards Ben Vorlich.

VIII

BY LOCHEARN TO ARDVORLICH

O it's up in the morn and awa' to the hill,
Where the lang simmer days are sae warm and sae still,
Till the peak o' Ben Vorlich is girdled wi' fire,
And the evenin' fa's gently in bonnie Strathyre.

HAROLD BOULTON

No wonder Scotland has a plenitude of lochs and
running waters. Doubtless it makes for beauty and
luxuriant growth—tall trees and lovely ferns nestled
amidst their tender mosses—but sometimes it palls
to find rain morning after morning, with no respite.

Here in Lochearnhead they laid full responsibility on the Lammas floods, and looked grieved
when I passed an obvious retort.

But rain or no rain, it certainly looked enchanting as I paused for a moment before taking the road.
The colour scheme, the whole vista, was exquisite.

The hotel was embowered in roses—the long
oval loch spread out in front, on either hand high
green hills, wrapped in their cloaks of mist. One
or two imposing laburnum trees, heavy with seed-
pods, formed a near-by background to the rose
hedge, and indeed the world looked very beautiful
to-day.

The swallows were flying low, hundreds of them
it seemed, and every moment I expected one at
least to immolate itself on the telegraph wires, but

just as disaster appeared imminent, a graceful swerve to safety, at express speed, and then the grand circle once more in seemingly endless procession.

As I took the ambling, twisting road by the loch-side, one after another the little white cottages, perched on a slightly higher level than the turnpike, were veritable bowers of roses and nasturtiums.

Loch Earn is almost on the path here so close is it, but so abundant is the vegetation that only an occasional glimpse reveals its shimmer.

The wayside bushes are weighed down with luscious rasps that no one seems to gather. Last summer when wandering amongst the by-roads near Forfar and Kirriemuir I noticed the same thing. Literally miles of bushes almost at the breaking-point so heavy was the fruit, dropping to rot on the ground.

A winding, turning road this, as loch-side roads should be, each bend disclosing new glories, each turn a different charm.

Off to the left is the gash called Glen Beich, and up on the rocky hill-side I spied a shepherd and three dogs. He was moving at surprising speed, a heavy bag on his back, and the dogs were the embodiment of energy. Suddenly one would detach himself from the moving group, obeying a command, and bound up the rocky side, in and out amongst the boulders, now lost to my vision, anon appearing a black moving dot on the green patch, and then a trickle of sheep descended at his will. It was wonderful work, and even at the distance formed a most interesting picture.

The setting on the right was now very beautiful —trees, heather and ferns, giving a colourful background of almost enchanting loveliness.

To botanist, naturalist, fisherman or mere lover of scenic beauty, here was a very paradise.

The sun was coming out again, and on the other side of the loch hills and glens were appearing as if by enchantment, while the background of mist, slowly rolling eastward, once again gave proof that Nature can stage-manage in the grand style !

I wanted a root of heather for my garden, and high above on a sandy bank was the ideal bush. As I gently inserted the spatula out it came—and then I found it to be literally alive with ants. But these were not its only tenants. A small, beautifully marked snake, some ten inches in length and in girth equal to an ordinary lead pencil, was nestling amongst the roots. It was too bad to dislodge so many citizens of the wild, so I gently replaced the root in its former position and left them, I trust, none the worse for my interference.

Once again Nature stage-managed a transformation. The hills disappear, hidden by a forest of larch, oak and fir. The road was almost dark in parts, adding a new beauty and charm to the way.

The larches here are conspicuously beautiful, and it set me wondering how to-day they form such an outstanding feature on so many western roadways, their introduction to our land being so recent.

Now, the little township of St Fillans, living on the outer edge of high, rocky hills, rugged and bare, to-day's mist adding infinity to the scene.

Opposite is the island where the Neishes thought they were secure, until " the lads were the lads," and a dire fate befell them.

In front lies the road to Crieff and the far North ; to bens which dwarf these hills, and glens whose loneliness is like an ache in the heart, so desolate and forsaken are they; but here too is peace and solitude, and to cross the narrow, hunchbacked bridge which spans the Earn at St Fillans is to leave the world behind for a space, so silent and deserted seems the path.

Busy motors may rush past on the high road to Crieff and the North—but here was a pedestrian's sanctuary, a care-free walking road.

Few motorists trouble one, and buses are forbidden. Here was indeed a haven where one could hold the crown of the road undisturbed.

Cool trees, green moss for a carpet, and the singing burn, crooning away to itself in an undertone, while just a few yards away (and by the same token some miles distant !) the rushing cars on the main road. But soon the burn is gone and the loch glitters and shimmers on the right.

The path is of surpassing beauty now, the bracken almost as tall as the high deer-fence which in parts guards the narrow roadway.

Trees meet overhead, and the loch is lost below as the road climbs upwards.

This is Ardvorlich country—what a setting for deeds of clan daring, and many a black act found its birth here.

Over there is Glenartney, where Drummond-

Ernoch was so foully used by the Children of the Mist, and this narrow, beauteous pathway leads past Ardvorlich, dark amidst a setting of trees as if seeking seclusion so that again such fearful visitants may be strangers to her door.

At the highest part of the roadway the trees fell away, and below stretched miles of loch, a huge plain of silver without a ripple or movement, or so it appeared from this vantage point. Down and round the bend, easy walking now, over a narrow bridge and once again the loch keeps company with the roadside. A musical lapping of the water, the faint rustle of trees accompanied a silence that was almost eerie.

Again the road mounts, but by such easy gradients as to be almost imperceptible until the loch appears sheer below, the steep bank a festoon of fern, oak and rowan. The rowans are early here, and the red berries add an extra splash of beauty to the canvas. Inland were trees, how far they travelled back before joining the hills I cannot say, but only here and there was a background visible, and an almost perpendicular wall of rock, moss-covered and hoar, veils a wider view. The hills I saw from the other side are lost now that I walk almost at their feet!

Just where the oak and rowan give place to a fragrant larch wood with a brown and inviting carpet, where one could idle and smoke but for the long miles ahead, a small weather-beaten stone stands alone and isolated by the loch-side.

It marks the place of interment of Major James Stewart, whose bones were afterwards removed to

the family vault at Dundurn, and who " died
about 1660."

I wove quite a romance for my own satisfaction
as I slowly proceeded along this larch-lined path,
as I take it this is the Major Stewart who slew
Kilpont, and whose birth was preceded by such a
fearful tragedy.

There are one or two varying accounts of the
Kilpont murder.

Wishart (according to Sir Walter Scott no very
reliable authority) describes how, early one dawn,
" before the drums had beat to march, the whole
camp was in an uproar, the men all running to
arms, shouting and storming like madmen in their
rage and indignation."

Montrose hurried to the spot, fearing trouble
between the Irish and Highlanders, when he found
Lord Kilpont's body lying on the ground, several
wounds providing full evidence that he had been
dirked. Kilpont was not the only victim, as
Ardvorlich had also stabbed the sentinel and made
his escape into the night.

Some said Stewart had been bribed by the
Covenanters to kill Montrose, and that on voicing
his intention to Kilpont, upon whose assistance he
relied, that officer was so horrified that Stewart
murdered him to close his mouth. Another theory
was that the murder was committed merely in hope
of reward. Probably both are wrong, but the fact
that Stewart made his way to the Whig army and
was given a high command by Argyle probably gave
rise to many stories.

The most likely version is that when Alaster

Macdonald, with some Irish auxiliaries, was on his way to join Montrose, they crossed Ardvorlich's lands and committed some outrage which he naturally resented. In addition to lodging complaint with Montrose he also had a violent scene with Macdonald, so much so that both were placed under arrest, it is said on instructions of Lord Kilpont.

To a man of Stewart's hot temper this was insufferable, and to avoid trouble and feud in his camp Montrose brought Ardvorlich and Macdonald together and forced them to shake hands and become, outwardly at least, once more on friendly terms. Stewart was such a powerful man that when he grasped Macdonald's hand he crushed it so as to make the blood start.

After the Battle of Tippermuir, when the army was encamped at Collace, Montrose entertained his officers, and naturally Ardvorlich and Kilpont were of the company! There is an old rhyme which says "Grace and peace cam' by Collace," but it was far wrong on this occasion.

Excited by drink, Stewart apparently upbraided Kilpont for his former action, and to men of their type words led to blows, and Ardvorlich in his anger stabbed his friend and then made good his escape. That he joined the Covenanting army means little. To a fighting man, fierce and resentful, continuance with the Montrose forces was impossible, and under the circumstances nothing was more natural than to put his services at the disposal of the other faction or alternatively be outlawed by both.

LOCH EARN

Afterwards in Lochearnhead they told me the tradition of the Major Stewart stone by the road-side—but I cannot vouch for it although it is likely to be founded on fact, as are so many of these old-time, bygone tales.

Major Stewart had an inveterate hatred of the MacGregors, and considering how he and his for-bears had suffered at the hands of that unruly clan, his animosity is not to be altogether wondered at !

In life he was a strong, virile, indeed ruthless man—quick to anger and ready to avenge insult, real or imaginary, to the full.

He had many opportunities of wreaking venge-ance on his hereditary enemies, and hanged and slew not a few MacGregors in his day.

That the Clan Gregor was not composed of weaklings history proves ; however, they were gener-ally worsted by the redoubtable Ardvorlich warriors.

When death—the one implacable enemy he could not resist—claimed Major Stewart, as the cortege was proceeding slowly by the loch-side, word was whispered that the MacGregors, robbed of vengeance when their enemy was in life, were gathering to wreak some unspeakable insult on his dead body. An emergency grave was dug by the road-side, and there he lay until, at a later date, his remains were taken up and laid to rest in the family burial-place ; and so in death, as in life, his enemies were foiled.

The story may or may not be true—I give it as it was related to me—but many more unlikely deeds were enacted in these old days when clan feuds were rife and passions carried sway.

But another discovery drove the thoughts of Major Stewart and his stormy life from my mind.

On the inland side of the path, amongst tall rank grasses, was another stone, weather-beaten and obscure. I could just decipher the inscription :

NEAR THIS SPOT WAS
RE-INTERRED THE BODIES OF
7 MACDONALDS OF
GLENCOE KILLED WHEN
ATTEMPTING TO HARRY
ARDVORLICH
ANNO DOMINI 1620

Here was glamour of old clan days with a vengeance. A restless, fighting sept the Glencoe men, but perhaps not much worse than some of their neighbours who dwelt in a greater, or at least more outwardly apparent, odour of sanctity.

Up there lies Ardvorlich itself, and through the trees I glimpsed two ponies, pannier-clad, with some attendants (the one in the kilt fitted into the picture ideally), walking quickly towards the house. They were beaters, and the long day on the grouse moors had apparently left them fresh and strong, because I should not care to go far at the pace they were making.

But if the men of Ardvorlich were not always on such peaceful missions, they lived in a district which was frequently the scene of warlike unrest, and it took strong men to hold their own amongst such neighbours.

At one time a stone called the Clach Dearg, in

the possession of the Ardvorlich family, had a wonderful reputation for the cures it was supposed to effect amongst sick cattle. Unlike modern remedies, each of which is limited in its scope, the Clach Dearg, or red stone, was alike good for all. It was simple too in its application, indeed one had merely to dip it in water, and after drinking, the diseased animal was certain to recover its health and energy. The legendary story of this talisman is, I think, that at one time it was used in some sacred rites by the Druids.

This sort of " charm stone," if I could so call it, was not altogether uncommon in past times.

In Glenlyon House they had also a stone which was even more powerful in its results. As a matter of fact if the water in which it had been immersed was affused over those going to feud or battle, it possessed the valuable merit of making them immune from serious wounds. As lately as the '45 this stone was produced, and the men going off to "fecht for Charlie" underwent its baptism. There was one exception, and he said it was not merely superstitious but actually sinful, and so refused to have the ritual performed on his person. He alone was killed ; all those so protected returned from Culloden unscathed !

No less wonderful was the cure for madness which was invested in a bone, at one time the property of Campbell of Barbreck; or the precious Lee Penny which performed many miracles in its time.

Quaint flotsam and jetsam these upon the troubled sea of Scottish history and superstition, but doubtless effective enough in their own way. Faith, it is said, can move mountains.

Nor was second sight confined to the Highlands, indeed Peden the Prophet was a Lowlander, and is there not a tale of another Ayrshire man who, stranded in London, far from home and loved ones, was told by some supreme agency to go home and dig in a certain spot and there he would find something to advantage him ? Doing so, he recognised the place spoken of by his spectral assistant, and digging as instructed, found a pot of gold which laid the foundation of a noble family !

This may seem all by the way, but in truth it is not so far from our subject either. Look back amongst the trees there and you will see the turrets of Ardvorlich " much resembling pepper-boxes," because this is the Darnlinvarach of " A Legend of Montrose," and here it was that Allan had the " cloud upon his mind."

Heather hills again stretch away on the left, and by now the road has deserted the loch, although glints of its sheen are visible through the thick foliage. On passing the gates of Edinample Castle, a gaunt white house amongst a bower of trees, perfect in its setting and admirable in its taste— the glistening miles of silvery water come into the open with a dramatic gesture.

> In the lone glen the silver lake doth sleep ;
>   Sleeps the white cloud upon the sheer black hills,
> All moorland sounds a solemn silence keep,
>   I only hear the tiny trickling rills.

From here the long vista of hill and glen on the

THE PASS OF LENY, CALLANDER

western side is majestic. The sun was going down and his dying glory formed such a picture that I stood in the rain—for strangely it was a constant and steady downpour on my side of the loch, but dry and bright on the other—loth to leave it all.

And so, down the short brae, past the little white church, and back to the Balquhidder road again.

IX

KINGSHOUSE TO CALLANDER

This is the road the clansmen trod,
   In the days of the long ago,
When a man was a man—and his own keen blade
   Was the ward of the way he would go ;
      When a man's sword arm
      Was his guard from harm,
And he walked as his own will bade !

IT was hard to believe that just over the hill-side
lay the dark and rugged Inverlochlarig. This
morning the sun was making amends, and if to-day
the beauty of the road was more domestic, it had
a full share of witchery and charm.

Yesterday in Rob Roy's glen it was bleak and
forbidding ; here near-by bracken runs to meet
the tree-clad slopes, splashes of colour relieve the
greenery, and altogether it was a blither road to
traverse this bright morning.

Even so, I do not know which road was better—it
is perhaps a matter of mood. Wooded slopes, tall,
nodding foxgloves, far heather stretches, charm the
eye and please the senses, but they cannot inspire
the heart with that feeling of awe which comes only
when one is alone amidst the stillness primeval and
desolate, of dark towering bens and tumbling
waters.

This fair roadway of to-day is Highland, but it is

domesticated. One instinctively knows that somewhere in front lie houses, shops, tourist hotels—yesterday led only to the wide-open, ben-ringed straths pathless and untrodden, where the red deer live, and the whirr of the grouse or the bleat of a sheep is all that ever breaks the silence. An occasional isolated cairn, its purpose forgotten ere its sentinel rowan was a sapling, was the only sign that foot had passed that way.

Here man has taken his place and wrestled with Nature until he has forced his will in parts. Hayfields cropped, but sodden in the August sun where the rains of yesterday form pools in the hollows. Some green, unhealthy-looking corn, poor fruit for such heavy ploughing, the eager bracken waiting a chance to overrun and claim once more its ancient birthright.

For a moment I paused to see if by chance old Ben More showed up against the waiting hills, and there, a yard or two in front, I spied a hill-sheep and a rabbit, noses almost rubbing, feeding off one small patch of green grass ! It formed an amusing picture, and one I wanted. Silently—or at least so I thought—the camera was adjusted, but when I looked up the rabbit had disappeared ! It was running no risks !

The day was hot now, bees humming about their duties, but not a bird note could be heard. August is the silent month amongst the feathered songsters, and but for a little brown wren which mysteriously flitted in and out of the hedgerow, of bird life there was no other sign.

Over on the right somewhere lay the old Balquhidder Church of yesterday, but I could not trace it amongst the wood-clad hills. It was a wonderful morning for day-dreams in the quiet heat, where but for a passing car the busy world might be non-existent.

The years cannot have brought many changes to these hills—and down the far-lying braes it would be no difficult thing to imagine the flash of a red tartan as Rob Roy or one of his sons adventured forth in peace or war.

Gone are the days when " to gang into Rob Roy's country was a mere tempting o' Providence." Time has long since broken that entail of evil which seemed fated to heir these hills and glens to sorrow and bloodshed.

Rob Roy was not by any means alone in the depredations of that day, but his name has come down to us, outstandingly because of the glamour Scott spread over him like a mantle, and of the times in which he lived—

> When tooming faulds or sweeping of a glen,
> Had still been held the deeds of gallant men.

The popular impression of a man who does deeds of prowess is of a great giant, upstanding amongst his fellows, but Rob Roy was not that. In fact he was not particularly tall, but he was gifted with two outstanding features which fitted him specially for his wayward, challenging life. These were his breadth of shoulder, which gave him power, and his extraordinary length of arm.

Think of the wonderful advantage a swordsman could claim whose arms were so long that he could tie his hose-garters below the knee without stooping.

Red as his name denotes (Red Robert) he was in many ways a braggart, but nevertheless a brave, valiant character to strive and survive as he did, his hand against so many implacable enemies. And in his wife he had a fitting mate, and Rob Roy on one occasion accused her of having caused most of his strife ! After all it is good that he lived ; his exploits and escapades have given an added interest to the grandeur of the hills and the beauty of the lochs and glens amid which his stormy days were spent.

It was difficult to believe that these serene and quiet uplands had resounded to the tumult of battle, and that hunted men had skulked from avenging blades amongst the rocks and bracken.

And now across the hump-backed bridge and through Strathyre, gay with scarlet geraniums and rambler roses, over the outward guardian bridge—and so again to the silent road.

Overhead the tall trees meet and the sunshine is lost for a space. Dark and sombre, but deliciously cool after the glare, the mossy banks are laden with ferns and the inevitable foxgloves range high amongst the bracken and tall grasses—and then the open road again, Loch Lubnaig shining and rippling in front, a sparkling silver sheet.

The mountains rise sheer from the loch-side carved from the solid rock, each with its banner of cloud, and a solitary angler plying his craft from a slowly moving boat is the only sign of life.

Here lived Bruce, the celebrated traveller, and

here he wrote his ponderous work on Abyssinia, running to five volumes no less, published towards the latter end of the eighteenth century. Near-by, the world first greeted Alexander Campbell, a poet and staunch Jacobite, who numbered Burns, Scott and Hogg amongst his distinguished friends. Not far away lie the mortal remains of Dugald Buchanan, the Gaelic poet mentioned elsewhere. The world has passed on, and they are forgotten by most, overshadowed by a more modern school, but mayhap they laboured not in vain!

Scott has, of course, overwhelmed all other associations with his " Lady of the Lake," and a setting of wondrous charm it is! The winding road holds by Lubnaig with its varied facets. On the left a garden of wild flowers is displaced by dense bracken, which in turn gives way to wood, here and there a patch of purple heather, amid which rocks and boulders add a sterner beauty.

I was told of a white wild cat which made its home somewhere near-by, and if true it probably by now adorns some " sportman's " smoke-room! Like the magpie and other so-called vermin, the wild cat, far from being extinct, would seem to be increasing in some districts. Owning no game preserves may account for my views, but I should be sorry to hear that the wild cat, badger and golden eagle had been finally exterminated and banished from their native haunts.

If Scott may be claimed as the literary giant of this district, Ben Ledi dominates it physically, raising his gaunt old head three thousand feet into the clouds, and peering over his neighbours from some uncanny angles. The name Ben Ledi signifies the Hill of God; and I sometimes think his huge bulk is more appreciated at a distance, for then he towers above the smaller bens like a Saul amongst the people!

In far back, forgotten days Ben Ledi was the stage of strange Druidical rites. There is no stone circle or monument to mark the occasions, but from its heights the people worshipped the sun, and this Beltane sacrament, if I may so term it, commenced on May Day and lasted for three days. Here was kindled the sacred fire, and doubtless many strange cantrips were indulged in by the priests.

When Campbell, in his wandering tour, visited this place, the boys still kept up the old Beltane-day customs.

He describes how these lads, gathered from the surrounding hamlets, met in some sequestered spot amongst the hills where the turf was thick and green. Here they lit a fire and cut a deep trench round it so that the inside formed a table; they then consumed a meal consisting of milk and eggs beaten into a custard. A thick oaten cake was then baked on the embers of the fire and divided into pieces equal to the number of persons. One part of the cake was bedaubed with ash or charcoal and then all the pieces were put into a bonnet. Each lad drew his cake, and he to whose lot fell the blackened section was deemed the victim or sacrifice to Baal's fire. Instead of being immolated, however, he was forced to jump three times through the embers of the fire, and that finished the ceremony.

Probably it is a relic of the old pagan days,

and perhaps by some such drawing of lots were the priests provided with human victims for their Beltane sacrifices.

Like the old Hallowe'en customs of a past generation, these things will soon be mere memories, so Anglicised are we becoming even in the country villages.

There is one dark legend associated with this grim old mountain, a tale more modern than its fire-worshipping devotees, awful if true, as I believe it is.

One winter's day a funeral party from the neighbouring Glenfinlas, numbering some two hundred mourners, was slowly wending its way to the graveyard of St Bride. They were crossing the mountain shoulder, white with snow, and under the belief that the ice was strong enough to carry them, or whether deceived by the snow, they proceeded across the small loch which graces the hill-side. When fairly upon its bosom the ice gave way and the whole company perished in the icy waters, Lochan-nan-corp, or the Small Loch of the Dead Bodies it is named to this day !

Dark thoughts these this bright noon, but in keeping with the rugged, cruel-looking hills hereabouts—and then the Pass of Leny took me and the mountains were for the moment obscured.

The Falls of Leny are amongst the show places of our land, and grand they doubtless are—but give me the Falloch in spate ; dashing amongst the rocks, foaming from the glen, the rowans red above and the nearest township a clachan !

You may not share my view, but be that as it

may, the wild free braes on the left are more interesting to me. Their untrammelled, natural beauty is portrayed in one of Scott's stanzas, and line for line they comport to it like a word painting :

> Boon nature scattered, free and wild,
> Each plant or flower, the mountain's child.
> Here eglantine embalmed the air,
> Hawthorn and hazel mingled there ;
> The primrose pale, the violet flower,
> Found in each cliff a narrow bower ;
> Foxglove and night-shade, side by side,
> Emblems of punishment and pride,
> Grouped their dark hues with every stain
> The weather-beaten crags retain.
> With boughs that quaked at every breath,
> Grey birch and aspen wept beneath ;
> Aloft the ash and warrior oak,
> Cast anchor in the rifted rock,
> And, higher yet, the pine-tree hung
> His shattered trunk, and frequent flung,
> Where seemed the cliffs to meet on high,
> Its boughs athwart the narrowed sky.

An old castle stood somewhere hereabouts, but in 1737 the stones were removed to build a mill and form a damhead ! It was a stronghold of the Buchanans, and probably was at that time a mere tumble-down ruin, as the Charter of the family dates back to 1247 in the reign of Alexander II.

This same Pass of Leny has been the scene of many an exciting incident, and here at Kilmahog one outstanding deed of prowess was performed.

It is an old traditional story that one Shaimis Beg, or Little James, so designated for his lack of inches, had a stronghold on the West of Loch Achray, where he was wont to retreat in times of danger or emergency.

This Shaimis Beg was keeper of the King's deer forests of Glenartney and Glenfinglas, and one day a band of Argyllshire Campbells, on some marauding excursion, made a descent on the royal preserves and killed a goodly number of deer, without so much as asking Little James's permission !

As the Campbells were returning from the chase, carrying the choicest parts of their spoil and on the outlook for somewhere to pass the night, they met Little James.

Strong in their numbers, and misjudging the royal warden because of his lack of inches, one of the marauders, pointing to the hut or stronghold on the loch, asked what magpie had built its nest on the island ?

Little James, no whit abashed, retorted it was the nest of one that scorned all greedy hawks, no matter from which quarter they came !

" Tell the magpie from us," returned the Campbell, " that we shall return and harry his nest ; tell him also that we shall return soon, and perhaps he will find that our hawks are good at taking their prey."

" Then," said Little James, not to be outdone in badinage, " it may so happen that the magpie whose nest you would molest may have power over many hawks which inhabit these mountains and glens, and when the strange hawks arrive it may be for their discomfort."

With that the Campbells resumed their journey,

taking their booty with them, as the warden without aid was powerless.

In due course the Campbells kept their promise, but Little James was on his guard, and calling out the men over whom he had authority, they put up such a stout defence that few of the invaders were allowed to return to their homes.

Amongst those who distinguished themselves in this scrap was one of little James's henchmen, by name Broilan Beg Macintyre, so named because of his diminutive size but vast fighting qualities.

The Campbells who escaped from the affray vowed to be avenged on Little James and all who swore fealty to him, but more particularly on Broilan Beg Macintyre, whose blade had inflicted such punishment.

Accordingly, five picked men of the clan set out to waylay Macintyre, and having crossed the Teith somewhere in the Pass of Leny they met the man himself, busy with his cattle, near the old bridge of Kilmahog.

Macintyre was alone and without arms, whereas the Campbells had bows and arrows on their backs and broadswords at their sides.

Evidently they did not recognise Macintyre, and one of them asked, civilly enough, if he knew of such a man and where he was to be found ?

Their victim replied that he did know Broilan Beg Macintyre and thought he could put them on his track, but feigning to be simple-minded, pointing to their bows and arrows, he asked what they were and for what purpose did they use them ?

The Campbells jeered and laughed at him, and

one of the party, handing him his bow told him to shoot. Macintyre, who in reality was a skilled bowman, acted so clumsily that his arrow merely travelled a few yards in wavering flight to the infinite amusement of the Campbells, who thought him a buffoon. But Broilan Beg was no fool, and picking the arrows one by one from his foeman's quivers, he was content to thole their loud laughter so long as he was gaining his point.

Only too late the mockers found their last arrow sped. Then Macintyre suddenly ran swiftly to the spot where he had directed the greater number of arrows.

Quick as the Campbells were to follow and rectify their error, Macintyre was faster, and ere they could come up to him three of the party were transfixed with their own shafts.

The surviving couple made off and left Broilan Beg Macintyre to tend his kyloes in peace !

To the right leads the road to the Trossachs, beautiful and worthy of a visit of exploration, but to-day it was not my road, cool and tempting as it appeared.

Above, the sky was like sapphire, broken here and there by white translucent clouds, and the smell of peat-reek from a near-by cottage lent an added charm. Indeed the whole atmosphere was delightful and vaguely unreal.

> All in the Trossachs glen was still,
> Noontide was sleeping on the hill.

Many years ago the Loch Katrine district charmed me—to-day I leave it unvisited. Last time I ventured it was in the hands of vandals—a cement pier or something of the sort was under construction and the beautiful loch-side was lacerated and dishevelled. Now I fear to go back, preferring to carry the memory of an enchanted spot, once opulent in its finery, and, beautiful as it still may be, defaced and pillaged by those who forgot their sacred duty to posterity.

The Highland temperament is complex, and an example is to be found in one, Malise Graham, who dwelt and had his habitation near Loch Katrine many generations ago.

In the early days of the seventeenth century a gentle name was no guarantee of wealth, and the precincts of Holyrood House were a debtor's sanctuary.

Somewhere about the year 1680 the Earl of Menteith betook himself to the capital to escape from a dunning creditor, until in despair he sent a messenger to Malise Graham beseeching his financial assistance.

Prompt to the call, Graham put the required amount in a roe-skin purse and set off on foot to the relief of his chief. Arriving at his lordship's residence, dusty and travel-stained, the lowland retainer who answered his summons, mistaking Graham for a beggar, was handing him a copper when the Earl, who happened to observe the incident, hastened to chide the man for perhaps giving offence to his kinsman, but Graham, far from being angry, drew the purse from his bosom and handed it to Menteith, at the same time observing that while he hoped the money would relieve his lordship's embarrassment, on his part he was never above taking a bawbee, and indeed would not object to take as many as the man cared to give him !

Over there at Loch Vennacher there is a tradition of a Kelpie. The Kelpie is a mythical demon in the form of a water-horse, and many are the Highland tales which surround the breed. In this incident the demon ingratiated itself with some children playing near-by, until one, more hazardous than his companions, mounted the horse's back. Soon the bolder spirits followed their companion's example, until one by one they were all astride. The artful Kelpie, with diabolical cunning, elongated his body to accommodate them all, but they, poor innocents, did not apparently observe the phenomenon ! Once they were all aboard as it were, the Kelpie suddenly plunged into the loch, where in a far cavern it devoured them at its leisure !

The story, so far as I can gather, was vouched for by one little boy who managed to escape just as the fearsome steed was on the point of plunging into the dark waters.

The water-bull was firmly believed in at one time in the North, and I think it was sometimes angled for, the bait being a sheep and the rope which served as a fishing-line was attached to a tree for security. Dr MacCulloch once came across a farmer actively engaged in pursuit of one which he believed tenanted a certain pool. His two sons were stirring the water with hay-forks while the farmer stood by with his gun, ready to shoot. As the water-bull was impervious to anything other than silver, the gun was loaded with a silver sixpence !

But here we are at Callander with its trim villas and colourful gardens, so well watered under its weeping skies.

The old Dreadnought Inn, at one time a notable landmark, has lately been demolished. The name originated from the MacNabs, whose motto it is. The stage from Stirling had its headquarters here, until railways were instituted, and even in the days of Scott, Wordsworth, Southey, and other celebrities who lodged at varying times in the old hostel, access to the wild country by the Pass of Leny was a hazardous journey. To-day the motor-buses splash one with mud as they pass, and if the Buchanan clan dared send round the Fiery Cross and appear accoutred with targe and claymore, the local constable at Kilmahog would fearlessly beard them armed with only notebook and pencil, and they would be lucky to get off with a caution for committing a breach of the peace !

X

CALLANDER
AND A GALLANT COMPANY

Quoth he, " If men had only tails,
They're near as guid as dogs, O."
DR NORMAN MACLEOD

ALL night it had poured incessantly, but this morning the sun, if a trifle wan and clouded, was doing its best to make amends and brighten things up a bit. Even so it did not look too full of promise.

Not merely had it rained during the sleep hours, but all the previous evening a weary, steady drip had saturated the country-side and made hills and crops alike sodden.

Out-of-doors it had been too uncomfortable and depressing for exploration, and so my only venture was to cross the street in search of newspapers and a book.

Newspapers there were aplenty, but of books the selection was not one which appealed to me, until I found a popular edition of an old favourite, one I had read and re-read several times. It may have been coincidence, perhaps I was on the verge of second sight, through wandering so much of late among the glens,—whatever tempted me I cannot say, but the book I bought was " Owd Bob," that epic of sheep dog trials. And so the evening

PENNING THE SHEEP, CALLANDER

became a pleasure as once again I entered into the rivalry of these two canine wonders, the proud, debonair Gray Bob of Kenmure and Adam M'Adam's outlawed, relentless Red Wull.

As I say, what tempted me to buy this book I do not know, but this morning, filling a pipe, I sauntered towards the hotel door, suddenly to become conscious that unusual doings were afoot.

The normally quiet, almost sleepy station yard was abustle with life. Farmers, shepherds, men of the hills and open spaces, were passing singly and in groups, and every man seemed to have at least one dog following closely at heel!

Never was the quiet street so thronged, and obviously something of importance was brewing.

And then the hall-porter told me all about it! The National Sheep Dog Trials were to be decided, and to-day so many dogs would qualify to represent their country at the International Meeting in the autumn.

No wonder there was an air of repressed excitement, and I hoped for the sake of these fine dogs that the threatened rain would hold off. But no— down it came with hurricane force, although well I knew that no deluge could damp the ardour of such a gathering.

Rain or no rain the contest would go on; and come wet or shine I too was determined to witness the sport.

We had not far to go, as the arena was a large field on the immediate outskirts of the town. The clouds were doing their worst now in a continuous heavy downpour; underfoot was little better than

K

a swamp, while a miniature loch in the centre of the field was visibly widening, yet everyone, contestants and spectators alike, appeared happy and unconcerned !

Than Callander there is no more appropriate arena for sheep dog trials, for it was in this district that the first South Country breed of sheep was introduced to the Highlands. The experiment was successful beyond all expectations, others followed the example, and the old breed was gradually superseded.

In 1759 an Alloa shepherd named James Yule had been unfortunate in respect to disease amongst his flocks, and anxious to try what a change of pasture would do, he sent twenty score of year-old lambs—hogs, I believe, is the proper term—to winter on the lands of a Mr Buchanan near Callander.

Two men, each answering to the name of Murray, introduced flocks, one in Glen Falloch, the other in Glendochart. Later, one Lindsay came to Lochearnhead, and so the system spread, the advent of the sheep tending to break down old customs and in great measure cause depopulation, with all the heartburnings and sadness caused by the clearances.

Writing somewhere about the last years of the eighteenth century, one of those old peregrinating journal-makers whose works are so interesting to-day, writing of the Western Highlands says :

" The spirit of speculation has spread rapidly from valley to valley. An epidemic of madness for sheep-grazing seems to rage with unabating fury. Rents within the last ten years have advanced beyond all former calculation ; most parts of the

Highlands are under sheep ; and the country has become desolate, and almost drained of its native inhabitants."

But the story of the clearances and the heartless dispersal of the moral owners of the glens is too sad a tale for this late day, and in any case here was gathered as cheerful an assembly as any man could wish to meet, Highland and Lowland in friendly contest.

A shepherd was working his dog when I arrived at the ringside. Blinding rain was lashing across the field, but his oilskin was lying on the grass at his side, and he was apparently too engrossed even to throw it over his shoulders.

And then followed a wonderful exhibition of man's training allied to canine sagacity.

It is all a matter of haste without flurry ; the man's pent-up emotion and excitement are not obvious, but are there nevertheless, as every moment counts.

Command and style are awarded valuable points, and the secret of success lies in quick under-standing between man and dog.

A whistle—and the sheep are heading straight down the course. Another whistle—on a different note—and Mirk or Rover sinks to the ground so that the speed of the five sheep is checked. It was all very wonderful—the pages of " Owd Bob " come to life !

Listen to this : " At the pen it was a sight to see shepherd and dog working together—the master, his face stern and a little whiter than its wont, casting forward with both hands, herding the sheep in ; the grey dog, eyes big and bright, dropping to hand, crawling and creeping, closer and closer.

" ' They're in ! Nay—ay—dang me ! Stop 'er ! —good Owd Un ! Ah-h-h, they're in ! ' and the last sheep reluctantly passed through on the stroke of time."

Change the idiom and there you have it, be it in Yorkshire dales or amongst West Highland hills.

What made it even more noteworthy, to me at least, was the fine work done under such distressing conditions. The rain was torrential with but few fair intervals, and the fairway was now quite under water. Time and again the sheep balked at the water, but the dog forced them on in a marvellous way.

I admired the men—hearty, open-air, good fellows—but I take off my hat to the dogs ! It was a competition—and a keen one at that, every man anxious to have the honour of representing his country at the even sterner trial in September— but never was rivalry conducted under more friendly conditions.

Dogs were here from all quarters of Scotland— from Campbeltown in the west, Berwick in the south, St Andrews upheld the honour of the east, and from Inverness a champion came to represent the north.

As for the men, widespread as were their homes, every farmer greeted his fellow as Tom, Sandy or James. It was an outstanding example of big, clean, open-air methods, and a joy to be in such company. In Doric or Gaelic it was all the same —broad humour, kindly jest—a handshake and a

" hard luck " for the man who failed to pen his
sheep in the stipulated time, or a hearty clap when
the work was done in smart, business-like style.

If the shepherds concealed their anxiety under
a show of indifference, not so the dogs! They
quivered with excitement when a rival was working
its trial, and their eyes never left the sheep, as if
each awaited the signal to " away bye " and show
the other fellow how to control his charges!

In front as I stood, the Leny was gradually rising—a rushing, dark-brown flood. On the right
towered Ben Ledi, a black, broken mass amidst the
clouds, one moment clear and dominant, soon again
screened and indistinct behind the mist and rain.

Slightly to the left of the great ben, and I hope
discernible on the photograph reproduced, is a huge
boulder which goes by the name of Samson's
Putting Stone.

Perhaps you do not know, but Samson at one
time lived with his mother in a hut on the hill-
side, and naturally his amusements were of a type
befitting his herculean strength.

One morning he lifted this great stone with the
intention of throwing it into the valley below, but
either he had not sufficient breakfast (which, as a
slur on his mother, I discard) or the stone slipped
from his hand and came to rest in its present, and
rather precarious, situation.

We are to-day puny mortals, but even Samson's
feat was child's play compared with that of Old
Nick, who once took a huge rock in each hand and
threw them at St Patrick. One is to-day Dumbarton Rock, on which stands one of Scotland's four

" official " castles, and the other is named Dumbuck, so that his missiles were no light pebbles. Fortunately St Patrick escaped between the two, and sought a more serene haven in Erin.

All that, of course, is by the way, and has nothing to do with sheep dogs and their more modern tasks.

By now everyone was thoroughly drenched, but such was their ardour that, like Tam o' Shanter —although from a vastly different reason—they

> Didna mind the storm a whistle.

For my part, I decided to take to the road again before I was thoroughly water-logged.

On my way back to Callander I passed a hayfield now quite under water, only the tops of the haycocks showing, and what before had been bare and comparatively featureless hill-side was now alive with churning mountain burns.

XI

ON TO STIRLING

The day is cold, and dark and dreary,
It rains, and the wind is never weary.

It was still raining, and in no uncertain manner, when I left Callander by the Doune road. Everything seemed water-logged, and the passing cars were splashing and adding to the already over-great discomfort.

Scotland is a beautiful country, but on a wet spell such as this its beauties are apt to be lost in the mists and haars, and it takes a very plenitude of beauty to atone for floods and spates.

However, I was on the road, rain had done its worst, and I was determined to keep to my programme, come what would.

The road was uninteresting until I came to a ruined cottage on the left. A small furry animal on the roadway was behaving in a curious manner. It would run about a third part of the way across, raise its head in a peculiar, peering attitude, reminding me of a miniature sea-lion, then turn and scurry back to cover. I halted a few yards off to watch what was brewing. It was, of course, a weasel, and was quite oblivious of my presence. After one or two attempts it ran to the camber of the road, lifted its young one and bore it towards the old cottage. The poor little one had been run over by a passing car and was crushed and lifeless. I am not an admirer of the weasel tribe, but I felt sorry for the hapless mother, cruel, blood-thirsty little beastie though she is !

I wonder when wild life will adapt itself to the swift-moving motor traffic. Between Callander and Doune I counted four small birds—all chaffinches, I think—and one dead rabbit on the roadway. Next time you happen along a country road keep a sharp look out, and the mortality will surprise you. It is, I suppose, unavoidable under modern conditions, but anyone who tramps the open roads must often regret the seemingly inevitable destruction of so much innocent bird life. Everyone knows how foolishly a dog behaves towards motor traffic, and there is some lack of understanding amongst even the most intelligent of animals in this respect. Still :

> I'm truly sorry man's dominion
> Has broken nature's social union,
> And justifies that ill opinion
> Which makes thee startle
> At me, thy poor earth-born companion,
> And fellow-mortal !

The road had been commonplace so far ; pretty in parts with its green braes and wooded parks, until after passing Burn-of-Cambus, when it rapidly changed in character.

The outlook was now altogether different. Away in front were great hills, and while the rain was still as persistent as ever, the sun was shining upon their peaks, and as I plodded through the mire they reminded me of the fabled house with the golden windows.

I marvelled at the number of magpies to be met with on the road. It is a beautiful bird, and appears to me to be developing into a larger creature than formerly. With the selling of estates and the reduction in gamekeepers and wardens, vermin—for in such category is this graceful bird classed—is not being kept in check, and hawks and weasels are on the increase. Anyone who frequents the open spaces will have noticed this.

These magpies were not scared, and kept about their business on the roadside until I was almost upon them, when they sailed rather than flew into the near-by branches and returned to the roadway ere I was well passed.

Fortunately for me there were five in the group I particularly noticed, because there is an old freit associated with the magpie, or the pyet as I knew it in my boyhood's days, which tells us :

> Ane is ane, twa is grief,
> Three's a wedding, four's death.

Skirting Doune the promise of beauty was rich. The woods were verdant and checkered with varying tones of green, and at the bridge spanning the Teith the spell of romance lay over all.

In front stands a white church and manse as if built to grace the spot, as indeed it does ; while on the left the castle of Doune made a picture too exquisite to pass without lingering over and for a time dreaming of other days.

The village of Doune was at one time a noted

centre for the making of pistols, and was indeed a warlike district in more senses than one.

Charles Mackie tells that when Prince Charlie reached Doune he was hospitably entertained by the family of Newton. Colonel Edmonston's sisters, dreading discovery of their guests by treacherous servants, personally waited on the Prince.

Their relations, the Edmonstons of Cambuswallace, were also present, and when the Prince was about to depart, having graciously held out his hand, after all the other ladies had kissed it, Miss Robina Edmonston of Cambuswallace, anxious to have a more special mark of favour, asked that she might " pree his Royal Highness' mou'." Charles, nothing loth, took her in his arms and kissed her "from ear to ear," to the envy and mortification of the other ladies present ! It is only fair to say that Chambers gives a slightly different version of this incident.

They were staunch Jacobites, the Edmonstons. One of the family carried the standard at Sheriffmuir, and the same gentleman once overawed Rob Roy.

James Ramsay of Ochtertyre recounted the incident to Sir Walter Scott in person, and so we may accept it as authentic.

There was some public celebration or occasion on foot at Doune, and amongst other festivities it was marked by a bonfire. James Edmonston of Newton was present, as was also Rob Roy. The famous outlaw had said or done something to give offence to Newton, and that gentleman ordered him to leave the scene or he would throw the MacGregor into the fire !

" I broke ane of your ribs on a former occasion," said he, " and now, Rob, if you provoke me further, I will break your neck."

Rob Roy is said to have suffered in prestige for taking the threat so quietly, but as Edmonston was an important man in the Jacobite party, and was doubtless surrounded by powerful friends, the MacGregor was probably wise in retiring.

It is unlikely that unless some such circumstances weighed the balance strongly against him that he who would not barter

> The wild deer's franchise for the heifer's thrall,

and whose whole life was a battle against superior odds, would slink off like a whipped dog.

A nephew of Rob Roy, Gregor MacGregor of Glengyle, or as he was known to the Highlanders, Ghlun Dhu, held Doune Castle for the Prince in '45. Although situated in such close proximity to Stirling with its Hanoverian Garrison, MacGregor occupied Doune for the insurgents until their return from England. The prisoners taken at the Battle of Falkirk were sent here, amongst them John Home, the author of "Douglas," who made his escape and afterwards wrote a "History of the Rebellion."

Here is an apposite verse from his pen :

> War I detest ; but war with foreign foes,
> Whose manners, language, and whose looks are strange,
> Is not so horrid, nor to me so hateful
> As that which with our neighbours oft we wage.

The verse, of course, has no connection with his own incarceration in Doune Castle.

As was to be expected, Scott knew this district well, and the castle figures in "Waverley," and to most its associations with Fitz-James are well known.

Romance and chivalry, fell deed and daring, have all played their part hereabouts, but the most intriguing tale of all was the revenge of an insulted tailor!

Doune was a favourite residence of Margaret, widow of James IV, and her tailor was one James Spittal. In his day the only way to get across the Teith was by means of a ferry, and the boatman was a thrawn type of Scot who, apparently, was a law unto himself. Arriving on the bank one morning the Queen's tailor found that he had no money on his person, and the ferryman refused to let him across. Notwithstanding his lack of small change Mr Spittal was in reality a wealthy man, and so by way of poetic justice he built the bridge and the ferryman was ruined!

The bridge was widened and repaired by the Road Trustees in 1866, but the stone bearing an inscription from the old bridge still survives. I could not properly decipher it, but in the centre there appears to be a pair of scissors, insignia and proof of the bold tailor's art!

Trudging along in the rain, it was a never-ending source of wonder to me how Nature orders her affairs during the seasons.

From experience I know that green and varied as the journey is to-day, it can claim no thrill of outstanding beauty, and yet in a month or two it will be transformed into a vista of enchantment. The hills will appear behind the quick shedding trees and will vie with each other in their shades of bronze, brown, russet and crimson. The dying bracken, blood-red in the distance, will run to meet the snow cap, and the whole will form an autumn scene I do not care to miss. The roadway will be carpeted in a deep, richly coloured mast, edged curiously with yellow pine needles. Unflinching old mansions, with an aura of romance about them, will appear where a month before no thought of such was apparent, giving an added interest to the scene.

The brilliant old cock pheasant, so startling amongst the green to-day, will merge with the tawny hues and become part of the colour scheme. That robin which is now so noticeable on the fern-covered dyke will be practically indistinguishable amongst the fallen leaves. As Fitz-Gerald sings :

> 'Tis a dull sight
>   To see the year dying
> When winter winds
>   Set the yellow wood sighing.

Fine thoughts these on this rain-sodden road, but prompted and presaged by the ripening hips and haws of the hedgerows.

Day dreams, however, were poor shelter from the persistent downpour, and even the leafy branches above were adding their drips now, their resistance having been sorely tried.

The hills on the left were dark and angry-looking,

as if they too were being tormented by their weight of cloud, and then I saw standing high and proud Stirling Castle. Presently the rain was, if anything, worse, but the grey old citadel appeared as if bathed in the evening sun. The trees concealed it again, and now was disclosed the Wallace Monument, stark and straight amongst its woods on Abbey Craig.

A good samaritan offered me a lift, but I was too wet to sit in comfort, and preferred to finish the last mile or two on foot.

Entering Stirling from this part is picturesque and impressive.

On the right the castle is strong and dominating, a landmark which can hold its own with every challenge; but couple it with the Wallace Monument on Abbey Craig upstanding against its background of hills—and then you have an entrance with which few towns can vie!

Look back now along the road you have come, until then rather restricted by the wayside trees and hedgerows, and you will find a serried row of massive bens, fantastic they looked in the half light, but overpowering in their bulk and majesty.

The great ponderous slopes tower to the skies and form a guard to the Western Highlands, and these same hills were not without their danger to the Lowland farmers in the old days when the restless clansmen were on the move. There is no little truth in the saying,

Forth bridles the wild Highlanders,

and old Stirling has withstood many shocks from

every airt and was deserving of all the natural protection she could possess. But if the heart is old, the branches are young and vigorous, and I know of no town where the suburbs are finer.

Every moment brought the grey old town a step nearer, and when I arrived it was to find the streets dry, the late sun strong and warm, everything bright and genial, until I could scarce believe that only a mile or so behind me the rainstorm had lasted all day, probably still raged, while here conditions were delightful.

As I passed beneath the solid rock, above, in the courtyard, I could see the kilted soldiers standing in groups on the scene of so many stirring incidents in the history of our land, and I fell to day-dreaming again and passed down the narrow street with a light step.

XII

STIRLING—
SCOTLAND'S BATTLE-GROUND

Old faces look upon me,
Old forms go trooping past.
W. E. AYTOUN

NEXT morning I was up and out of doors before sunrise.

Everything seemed grey and lonely. The streets were muffled in a thin early autumn haar which lay over and about the town and completely altered its appearance.

It had been my intention to explore the old-world spots before the douce citizens were out o' bed and about their daily business, but there was no one about to guide or direct.

It is a strange sensation to walk about the streets of a busy town and find all quiet and deserted.

The streets seem altered ; houses assume a new and unusual character, while the shops and business premises, with their drawn blinds and barred doorways, have a strangely desolate air.

Gradually the curtain of night was raised. The first audible sound was the note of a thrush. Then a sparrow chirped, and another, until the bird-world became clamorous and alive.

The white spectral mist gradually lifted, or rather

faded out, and from somewhere behind the hills an opalescent, pearl-pink sheen appeared and gradually increased in beauty.

Another day was born—just such a morning as most likely ushered in the days of long ago when the Roman Legions camped here, or the wild clansmen arose from their repose amongst the bracken.

Stirling looked very enticing in the early dawn. An occasional grey wisp of smoke from a chimney-pot, the sun glinting on a window-pane, spires and buildings emerging beneath the dominant old castle, clean-cut and strong, and behind, old ere man knew them, the mighty silent hills.

And now I knew that last night when I came to Stirling by the Doune road in the rain—to a town bathed in evening sunshine—beautiful as was the setting, I came by the wrong gate !

The proper way to approach this fascinating old town for the first time is by the South road. Come as you will, it presents a charming exterior, but come by the Glasgow road, and as you round the bend some three miles distant, the castle suddenly looms ahead, stark and dauntless, and in a moment you find your mind harking back to old warlike days when strong men in the pride of arms contested the road you tread.

But even so, and high and proud as the fortress stands, it is dwarfed by the bens which form its background. Away there dwelt the restless kilted warriors, ever ready to hold their own, and not averse to sampling the richer plains of the Lowlander, for Forth, notwithstanding its proverbial application, did not always " bridle the wild Highlander."

L

If you are fortunate, in that the bens are snow-capped and the forenoon sun is up and strong when you come, then you will see a panorama you are not likely to forget !

Still, come as you will, at once you realise that this is a town with a pedigree. Something tells you that here in the years gone by was hung the calendar of great days.

As in most county towns, there is a subdued atmosphere of assured position, hard to define but germane to the place. You sense that where to-day motor-cars park and buses ply, at one time clattered mounted men who rode on a king's business.

If I were to write a history of Scotland, I should take Stirling as my fulcrum.

History generally is a record of war, or the results of war, linked with selfish and scheming diplomacy, and those clustering old buildings were a hot-bed of such intrigues.

Centuries before the exploits of Wallace and the Bruce, the Romans knew this place. Queen Mary spent some infant years in the castle which cradled James II, James IV, and James V, and here, too, was crowned James VI.

An unfortunate name for a Scottish monarch—James. What tragedy overhangs the line—a fell black cloud of misery and woe !

Later, Bonnie Prince Charlie, with the hand of fate as always, turned against the Stuart race, played cantrips here on his way north to that fatal day on Drummossie Moor.

Yes : I would take Stirling as my centre, and from

there gather the threads of history and so trace my
heroes down the troubled years of the past.

Bannockburn ; Sauchieburn ; Stirling Brig ;
Sheriffmuir ; Kilsyth ; Falkirk — I do not write
them in chronological order but simply as they
crowd on the memory, and in these few, plucked
at random from the sheaf of time, is material for
many thrilling chapters.

Bannockburn forms a glorious chapter in our
national story, and on its battle-field was forged the
charter of our race, but to me the daring ruthless
day at Stirling Brig holds greater fascination. Moreover, had there never been a Stirling Brig, there
would have been no Bannockburn, but in any case
both were epic, and the two famous fields are
almost within sight of each other. Above all, I
love the fearless message Wallace sent to Warenne
when that English leader sent two clergymen to
offer terms if the little army of patriots would lay
down their arms. " Let the English come on,"
replied Wallace, " we defy them to their very
beards."

No room for doubt or misunderstanding there,
and when the invaders' men-at-arms heard the
defiant reply, they insisted on being led to the
attack.

The fighting leader of the English forces, a Scotsman, Sir Richard Lundy by name, and a skilful
general, realised the strong position of the Scots,
and hesitated to join the issue. The invaders
occupied the southern bank of the Forth, the Scots
army were on the north, and a narrow wooden
bridge was the only means of crossing.

Cressingham, the treasurer of the forces and a churchman, insisted that Lundy should advance at once, and, to do him justice, took his place in the van.

The English army then moved to the attack, and when about half were over and the other divisions were crowding on the south bank, impatient to cross the narrow bridge, Wallace gave the order, and the Scottish spearmen rushed headlong on the foe. The utmost confusion now prevailed, but soon the result was beyond doubt. Great numbers were slain by Scottish spears, and many were driven into the Forth to drown before their comrades' eyes. The invading army fled after destroying the bridge by fire to prevent pursuit.

Then followed one of those acts which, if true, reflects little credit on the victors. The proud and haughty Cressingham was slain in the first encounter, and so much was he detested by the Scots that it is said they flayed the skin from his body and made it into pouches.

Still, the Battle of Stirling Brig " was a famous victory," and as we look back, its true significance as the key-stroke to peace and freedom is at once apparent.

> High praise, ye gallant band,
>   Who in the face of day,
> With daring hearts and fearless hands,
>   Have cast your chains away.

The story of Sauchieburn is to me equally fascinating. Here father and son were in opposing camps, and it ended in the death of James III and the accession of his youthful heir, James IV

James III was never a fighting man, and although mounted on a wonderful charger, which it was said by the giver would carry him to victory or take him swiftly to safety, and armed with the famous sword of Robert Bruce, his heart failed him and he fled from the field.

The Bruce's sword, which in the hands of its original owner never failed or shrank from a contest, was afterwards found lying on the battle-ground, dropped in his haste or discarded in flight.

The craven monarch was riding for safety for the Forth, where lay the fleet under the gallant and loyal Sir Andrew Wood. He was unaccompanied, his friends and supporters being still engaged on the fateful field.

On passing a house, or mill, his spirited horse took fright at a woman who was carrying a pitcher of water, and threw its royal burden.

Stunned and shaken by the fall, clad in the cumbersome armour of the times, the King was unable to rise, and was carried indoors by the miller and his wife.

Feeling that his time was near, a condition perhaps more occasioned by nervous dread than physical disability, he asked his rude host to send for a priest.

" Who are you ? " questioned the miller.

" This morning I was your King," replied James, conscious that the day was lost and his reign at an end.

Rushing forth to find aid, the miller's wife spied some mounted men, unknown to her, in pursuit of the fleeing James. Accosting them, she explained her anxiety for the monarch and his wish for a priest.

" I will confess him," said one of the warriors; " lead me to his bedside."

When taken to the spot where James was lying, he approached with reverent air and questioned His Majesty if he could recover if immediate aid was forthcoming ? The King expressed the thought that he would, and the stranger, drawing his poinard, stabbed him to the heart.

The name or title of the regicide has never been revealed, and so this old-time battle of Sauchieburn, staged more than four hundred years ago, still cloaks its baffling historical mystery, now never likely to be solved.

Every chapter of Scottish history has its tale of stricken field or martial glory, and here is a cluster of such episodes.

In the old battle days Stirling must have formed a strong rallying point. Apart from the central fortress, Stirling Castle, there were within easy distance, indeed almost adjacent, amongst other keeps and strongholds, those at Doune, Robert the Bruce's at Clackmannan, Mar's Tower at Alloa, and Castle Campbell, the lowland seat of Argyll, which was ultimately razed by his implacable enemy, Montrose.

Romance states that the real name of Castle Campbell was Castle Gloom—that the Glen of Care flanked it on one side and the Burn of Sorrow on the other ; and that the castle looked down on the village of Dolour. Chambers was very wroth with Dr MacCulloch for accepting this story unquestioningly, and points out that Caer is not a Gaelic word and really means castle or camp; Dollor is merely *Dol or*, a high field; and the old Gaelic name for the stronghold was Coch Lleum or the Mad Leap, because of its precipitous position.

However, the old romantic description fits it admirably, even though " facts are chiels that winna ding," and so we must let it go at that !

Over there stands the Mote Hill :—

> . . . O sad and fatal mound,
> That oft has heard the death-axe sound,
> As on the noblest of the land
> Fell the stern headsman's bloody hand !

And some of his work would repay investigation too, as his was sometimes a busy profession in the days when a king's frown was a dangerous omen !

Almost five hundred years ago—in 1449 to be exact—James II acted as umpire when three chosen Scots tilted with three champions of France before an assembly of nobles and their ladies. To-day the motor-buses run near-by the tilting ground, and Stirling has a football team named King's Park.

It is all for the best, I have no doubt, and motor-buses and grand-stands are much more comfortable than accoutred chargers, or the pastime of the youth and beauty in the old dark days of sliding down a hill-side using an ox-skull for sledge.

As I stood at the wide corner place for a moment, the streets now busy with traffic, above the other sounds rose the peculiar drone of an aeroplane. It passed outwith my vision in a moment or two, swift and graceful, and as an every-day occurrence attracted little attention. And yet in Stirling, a stone's throw from where I stood, was made one of the world's first attempts to conquer the air.

The story goes back to the days of James IV, and was not a very successful affair for the braggart who made the effort.

The chief actor was an Italian friar who professed to be an alchemist, and so impressed the King that he had him created Abbot of Tungland.

Anxious still further to impress his royal master, he made it known that he had discovered the secret of flying, and a date being appointed for the display of his prowess, the King and his Court attended to witness the exhibition.

The Italian impostor did not lack courage, and fixing a huge pair of wings to his arms, he jumped boldly from one of the castle battlements. He fell heavily upon the rocks below, and was fortunate in that he broke only his thigh-bone !

If lacking in balance, his ingenuity was fertile, and as an excuse for this misadventure he gravely informed the amused spectators that his failure was entirely due to the fact that he had created his wings from the feathers of common barn-fowls, whereas he now saw that he ought to have selected only those of the eagle !

What is probably a deed of treachery and broken faith without a parallel was committed in Stirling Castle by James II.

That he was flouted by a section of his nobles who counted their station as above the law must be admitted, but the stain on his kingly honour is one which can never be erased.

Amongst the ruling families of Scotland, that of Douglas had always held high estate ; they were a sept feared by virtue not merely of their following, but also of the prestige of their fighting name.

In the reign of James II, when the fifteenth century was half run, Douglas had entered into a pact with two other powerful houses, represented in the east by the Earl of Crawford, and in the north by the Earl of Ross.

It was obvious to the King and his adherents that this triangular compact made the conspirators greater than the crown, and unless something was done to split them, the result might shake, if not destroy, the throne.

The Earl of Douglas was invited to meet the King in Stirling, and attended the conference with only a few of his followers, secure in the safe conduct given under the King's hand.

The Black Earl was received with every outward sign of friendship, and after supping with James and his chosen councillors, the King introduced the subject of the league Douglas had entered into with the Earls Crawford and Ross.

But the Douglas was not a man to be either bullied or cajoled, and he point-blank refused to repudiate the compact as his monarch wished.

To be bearded in his own council-chamber was more than the King's temper could support, and drawing his dagger he suddenly stabbed Douglas twice, exclaiming, " If you will not break this league, I shall ! "

Sir Patrick Gray and his fellow-courtiers soon completed the work, and the reeking body was thrown out of the window of what is to this day known as " the Douglas Room."

It was an unpardonable and an unkingly act, and was followed by bloodshed and war, which lasted for three years, until the King's forces triumphed over the rebel Douglases at Arkinholm in 1455.

A few weeks after the Douglas murder the new Earl, accompanied by six hundred fighting men, marched on Stirling and openly defied the King.

The letter of safe conduct which should have protected the slain Douglas was dragged at a horse's tail through the streets, and the town was pillaged and set on fire.

Stirling town has been plundered and sacked more than once since that date, but the last time it suffered in this manner was when the Highland army helped themselves to anything they fancied on their way north before the advance of Butcher Cumberland.

Never again is the old citadel likely to fire a gun in anger or be called upon to stand the rigour of a siege, but indeed it has played its part in the history of a nation, and so is entitled to rest and brood on the storied past, rich in a dowry of song and tradition, story and romance.

Lennox, while Regent of Scotland when the King was a child of five years, held a Parliament in Stirling. It is a striking commentary on the times that this callow laddie, King as he might be, was compelled to attend the proceedings, and a not uninteresting fact that there was a hole in the roof of the building in which the Parliament sat!

Naturally, the royal child was bored and restless,

more given to looking about him than listening to the heavy oratory.

His wandering eye soon spied the vent in the roof which held his attention, so that when Lennox, who, by the way, was his paternal grandfather, resumed his seat on the conclusion of a doubtless ponderous and lengthy speech, the child-monarch innocently remarked, " I think there is ane hole in this Parliament."

His prattling remark was prophetic. Some days later, ere the parliamentary session was concluded, the town was in the hands of the Queen's party, Lennox was dead, and the Earl of Mar was Regent in his stead !

But kings and princelings do not have it all their own way in the annals of this old town. John Knox, that dauntless theologian, preached in Stirling, I think at the coronation of James VI, then an infant, and many another great divine has expounded his doctrine to the citizens since that great reformer's day.

Not the least interesting wearer of the cloth was the Rev. John Russell, who " got his kale through the reek " so richly from the pen of Robert Burns.

While a slightly older man than the poet, Russell survived him by several years, indeed was still in the flesh when Waterloo was won, and he must frequently have had cause to regret the hall-mark stamped upon him by the invective of the Bard.

" Black Jock " was one name he would never escape, and generations yet to follow will know him by the title. As Russell was amongst the most bigoted and intolerant of the " Auld Lichts," his castigations were doubtless more than earned.

Professor Wilson recalls that he was one day walking in the vicinity of Stirling Castle. Unknown to the Professor " it happened to be a fast day," which in those times was given over to preaching and meditation, when he heard a noise which, to quote his own words, was " to be likened to nothing imaginable in this earth but the bellowing of a buffalo fallen into a trap upon a tiger, which, as we came within half a mile of the castle *we discovered to be the voice of a pastor engaged in public prayer*." The italics are mine. Professor Wilson adds that " his physiognomy was little less alarming than his voice, and his sermon corresponded with his looks and his lungs, the whole being, indeed, an extraordinary exhibition of divine worship."

That was " Black Jock " at his daily avocation, and by all accounts well might Burns write of him :

> But now the Lord's ain trumpet touts,
>   Till a' the hills are rairin',
> An' echoes back return the shouts,
>   Black Russell is na sparin' ;
> His piercing words, like Highlan' swords,
>   Divide the joints an' marrow;
> His talk o' Hell, whare devils dwell,
>   Our vera " sauls does harrow,"
>   Wi' fright that day.

Kilmarnock, indeed, must have been a quieter and better town to reside in when the Rev. John Russell decided to leave the " wabster lads " and remove his bull's voice and frenzied personality to Stirling.

A hundred years before Russell's time Stirling boasted another quaint theologian, by name Hunter, who appears to have been minister of the second charge. At least the first minister, a Mr Munro, along with the provost of the town, charged Mr Hunter with drunkenness, indeed in the outspoken manner of the times there was no beating about the bush, and they plainly stated that he had already consumed so much liquor that "at the sacrament he was under the influence of drink." The Bishop suspended him, and his subsequent doings are unknown save that in his old age he married a girl, daughter of a gardener.

From ministers to "grace before meat" is an easy transition, and Cheviot, that industrious collector of proverbs and out-of-the-way lore, is sponsor for the following:

It appears that at a dinner held in Stirling Castle no one present was able or willing to "ask a blessing" on the meat, and so the Earl of Airlie's footman was ordered to perform the office. At once the man, who obviously was a witty fellow and was doubtless called upon for that reason, without hesitation recited:

> God bless King William and Queen Mary,
> Lord Strathmore and the Earl o' Airlie,
> The Laird o' Bamff and little Charlie.

There is another version of the grace given by the same authority, which reads: "Bless these benefits, and a' them who are to eat them; keep them from chokin', worrying, or overeating themselves; and whatever their hearts covet, let their hands trail to them."

As I write, Stirling is in the throes of a ghost scare, one of those silly experiences none too uncommon of late years in various districts.

Last night the ghost appeared in the backyards of Middle Craigs, a white, spectral figure with outstretched arms, but before the civilian watchers and the police had gained entrance to the yard, with a distinct shuffling of feet—an unusual accompaniment for spectres and apparitions—the ghost had eluded the pursuers and completely disappeared.

But the whole of the old town is haunted. You can feel it in the atmosphere, the ancient buildings and the black battlements of the castle above, and it would never surprise me to see a gallant figure, in strange garb of other days, come down the crown of the causeway, sword in hand.

The playing children have gone indoors now, and the streets are surprisingly quiet and deserted. Stand here at the castle foot and let your imagination run riot for a spell as the sun goes down and a bat flutters past. What a motley procession to conjure with—kings, queens and princelings—all the royal blood of Scotland, grave or gay, have passed along here at some time in their checkered career.

The figure slipping by in the half light is a King, James V no less, but known to-night as the Guidman of Ballangeich, off in search of illicit pleasure and amatory joys amongst the peasant-folk outby. An English warden goes his rounds, anxious to see that all is safe ere retiring for the night. The skulking figure in the shadow is a spy from the desperate band of the lion-hearted Wallace, who is determined to drive the invaders forth across the border or die in the attempt. A gay cavalcade of knights and ladies fair passes on prancing steeds or caparisoned jennets making for the jousting; Knox with his fanatical bearded face and warnings of evil and woe; a Prince, the last of his race to seek a throne, shot at from a stronghold by rights his own. The history of our land unrolls in pageant form, because here is the old heart of centuries gone, the anvil on which Scottish deeds were forged.

The white silent haar of the morning was creeping back again, blurring the hills and enfolding the carse, and gathering round the castle hill it enshrouded the old historic stage where deeds were done which will live while Scotland breathes, and with a last look at the staunch old relic I made for the busy main streets where blue-clad policemen regulate the bus traffic, and the modern world thrives.

XIII

AN INCONCLUSIVE JOURNEY

> There's some say that we wan,
> And some say that they wan,
> And some say that nane wan at a', man;
> But one thing I'm sure,
> That at Sherra-muir,
> A battle there was, that I saw, man.

I⊤ all came through a chat with a fine old gentle-man who was sleeping in the Stirling hotel on his way north. Who or what he was I do not know, but he was a genial soul, garrulous to a fault, and I was glad to foregather with him !

We sat at the fire and smoked, and he told me how, many years before, he had explored the Sheriffmuir district while spending a holiday in Dunblane, and found it fascinating and teeming with interest.

I had, of course, read about the Battle of Sheriff-muir, pondering how the Stuart faction, had they possessed one lion-hearted, resolute leader, might easily have altered the history of our land. I had many times passed the road leading to the battle-field, but it looked so uninviting that I had never been tempted to explore the place.

The '45 and the personality of Bonnie Prince Charlie so dominate the Stuart cause and overshadow the preceding Jacobite risings and intrigues, that I had taken this battle for granted.

Now, sitting here chatting about it with an elderly English wayfarer, my interest was whetted by his tales and experiences, and I decided to devote my last free day for some time to come to this high-lying battle-field.

We sat late, and he told me of some ancient stones, each with its story, and none of which, according to his theory, should be missed by any man who wants to know something of his native lore !

The stones did it. I determined, come what might, fair weather or foul, to see those ancient landmarks, and to see them next day !

The sun was high as I left Stirling by the North road. The old bridge across the Forth—cousin-germane to that other and more famous brig which spans the Ayr—was a reminder of other days, and it pleased me to fancy that Argyll might have led his red-coats by this crossing to their camp at Dunblane, where they lay, before the clash of arms, that November day more than two hundred years ago.

Immediately in front rose the Abbey Craig with its great shelf-like broken side, once the vantage ground of mighty Wallace, and now crowned with his monument.

Across another narrow bridge at Bridge of Allan and the roadway climbs north. Pause for a moment at the summit and the Carse of Stirling is spread beneath like a great arena, pent by hills and mountains, with the castle rising straight

M

from the plain and dwarfing the clustering town into insignificance.

So under the tree-hemmed roadway to Dunblane, a town of great antiquity, which has played no unimportant part in historical and ecclesiastical directions.

It dates from Culdee times, and boasts a cathedral which was founded about 1140 by King David I. Like other sacred edifices it suffered in its time from the vandals, and a mob from Perth, under the leadership of Argyll and others, overthrew the altars in 1559.

Tannahill has made the name widely known to many, and given it a niche in poetic fame with his beautiful song, " Jessie, the Flower o' Dunblane."

The sun has gone down o'er the lofty Ben Lomond,
    And left the red clouds to preside o'er the scene ;
While lonely I stray in the calm simmer gloamin',
    To muse on sweet Jessie, the flow'r o' Dunblane.

Some authorities claim that the original Jessie is buried in the churchyard here, while others say that she existed only in the poet's fancy.

In the time of the '45 an Amazon of a heroic mould lived here, a servant-maid whose affections were all for the " King o' the Highland hearts." She was so incensed when Cumberland's troops passed through the village on their way north that, from an upper window, she emptied a pot of boiling water over their heads !

Tradition has it that it took some persuasion to prevent the red-coats from setting fire to the town in reprisal !

There are two or three interesting roads to Sheriffmuir—one a mere path—but my friend of last night mapped this adventure, so I followed his plan.

At once the broad North road, with its rush of motor traffic, was behind me, and the rutted, undulating country lane—for it is little more—led direct to the hills beyond.

The moss-covered stone dykes were a-cluster with hartstongue ferns, and notwithstanding the bright sunshine, everything looked damp and water-logged. After the first dip from the main highway the heavy path seemed to climb interminably, until suddenly the moor spread out in front and on every side the dying heather stubbornly contested the pathway. So quick indeed was the transformation that the wild desolation of the place was abrupt and unexpected.

In front stretched the heathery waste, in places jet black against the farther greens and browns. Here and there dark clumps of fir added a more sombre note to the whole, lent a strangely mournful beauty which somehow seemed in keeping with the atmosphere and the all-pervading silence.

Back towards the west by the road I had travelled ranged mountain behind mountain ; each white-topped ben seeming mightier than his fellows until clouds and earthly giants merged—the farther hills towards the north cloaked in snow.

Now for the first time I was conscious of a biting wind carrying an occasional sudden blash of rain, and was fain to shelter for a moment behind one of the butts which ran across the moor as far as vision carried. Anxiously I scanned in every direction—but no sign of fabled stones I had come to inspect, and by now the brightest of the day was behind.

A heron winged clumsily past, and I followed towards a struggling pine wood which guarded the sloping moorland, hoping that there, might be concealed the giant boulders so graphically described overnight.

The place seemed alive with game birds. A cock-pheasant rocketed away from almost under my feet ; grouse were more than abundant, but the few isolated farm-houses were too distant to afford guidance, and of man there was no sign.

Last night it had all appeared too easy—you went by such and such a farm and took a certain path to the right or left and the treasure was there for the taking, but somewhere I had gone wrong, and now the position seemed absurdly confused.

There was one stone in particular I had really wanted to see, because there a terrible deed was committed, almost pagan in its rites, shortly before the Argyll and Mar forces joined in battle.

My story of it was that one of the clans, anxious to propitiate the fates, insisted that their clay-mores should be blooded ere going into battle.

As there were no prisoners in the Mar camp, a man who was believed to sympathise with the Argyll whigs was taken from a near-by cottage, and the band in turn transfixed his body with their weapons, and then, satisfied that all would now go well, marched off to their allotted position in the battle-line !

A " Muckle Stane " marks the spot where this atrocious deed was committed, but I had missed my bearings, and the ghastly landmark was not apparent.

Somewhere, too, are " Seven Stanes " which might well be mistaken for the scene of no less noteworthy incidents in Druidical times, but really marking the scene of a " great battle " fought between William Wallace and the English invaders generations before the more modern affair which takes its name from Sheriffmuir.

Somewhere here on this lonely, dark moor, Wallace, learning that his Southron foes, to the number of 10,000 men, were marching from Stirling, divided his force into three divisions and hid them in the moss holes and gashes with which the terrain abounded.

Unaware that the Scots were even in the district, the English army straggled along without serious formation, and were surprised and furiously attacked from three sides. There followed a dreadful scene of carnage. The hatred between the countries was such that no quarter was given, and the invading forces were butchered to a man, with trifling loss to the Scots.

To mark the occasion Wallace had the " Seven Stanes " erected, a grisly monument to his prowess.

Well, here was I, standing on this desolate winterbound moor, dreaming of old-time battles and looking for stones that marked their site, while the sun was gradually sliding down behind the hills and the sky was taking the colour of lead.

And then came one of those things which " just happen."

Where he came from, or who he was, I do not know, but a man stepped out of the old fir wood just like some knight of old. The two features which impressed me were his hawk-like face and the monocle which dangled from a black ribbon. Still, he was my last hope, and I strode across the pine-needles and cones and told him my troubles and doubts.

" Stones," he said, and I wish you had been there to see his flashing eye and the sarcastic turn of his lip. " Stones—certainly there are stones, as you say, but what you call tradition is all trash and nonsense.

" There is no truth in the stories we are told to-day, sir—none ! If you are an Englishman go down there," and he pointed along the road I had part-way come, " go down there to the inn and buy a half-bottle of whisky, and you can have any number of tales told so long as it lasts ! If you are a Scot leave all that alone—it is worthless and traditional only."

Never have I met such an irascible man—and yet so kindly in his anger ! One thing anyhow emerged—there was an inn " down there," and so, thanking him, I made off, realising that I had taken the wrong airt at the cross-roads !

Everything seemed strangely silent. Now and again a lonely fir nodded as I passed—the empty butts spoke of life of an intermittent sort, but animate things had bedded for the night and only the flaming, lambent lights in the west broke the leaden gray.

When at last I reached the inn it was getting dark—that quiet, shadowy lack of light which steals across a moor—not the jet blackness of a town.

The stones were there—vouched for—not standing as the old strong men had left them in the long ago, but still marking the place where the conflict had been waged.

No : it would not be wise to go over the moor and see them. They were there all right, and their shadowy silhouettes were pointed out in the gathering darkness, but the moor was soaking and it would be better to come another day.

This was wisdom—the knowledge of the local which no sane man flouts, and so but for the recumbent shadowy outlines the " Seven Stanes " still eluded me !

Here was fought Sheriffmuir, a battle which surely stands out as one of the most remarkable episodes in British history.

Both sides claimed the victory, both leaders were unsoldierlike in the handling of their forces, and as someone said, if Dundee had been alive and in command of the clansmen the Whig army might have been annihilated. As it was, the right wing of each army crushed the opposing left wing, but the victory really rested with Argyll, bad as his leadership was.

As always when fight or foray was afoot, the MacGregors were in the affair too.

Rob Roy was in command of a considerable band composed of his own clan and the M'Phersons.

By inclination and sympathy the redoubtable

outlaw was all for Mar, and he took his place amongst the kilted faction. On the other hand, loyalty to his patron, Argyll, forbade that he should draw steel against him, and so here we had the peculiar incident of a body of armed fighting men ready to take their place in the battle-line, and yet inactive because their leader would not give the word.

It is said both Mar and Argyll sent urgent messages to Rob Roy asking him to do his part for them, but he coolly responded that if neither side could win without his aid, they could not gain victory by it. His hot-blooded followers were anxious to rush into the fray, but Rob forbade them, and indeed the M'Pherson leader, although under MacGregor's orders, had a heated altercation and nearly came to blows on the point.

When the battle was over Rob and his men, with great impartiality, gathered the spoil from both sides and returned to their native fastness, probably well satisfied with the part they had played !

Rob Roy there stood watch on a hill, for to catch
    The booty, for aught that I saw, man :
For he ne'er advanced from the place he was stanced,
    Till no more was to do there at a', man.

It is well that the MacGregor's reputation can stand even such a lapse as that ; his conduct on this occasion may be condemned, but his courage was undoubted, and it was an understood thing that spoils went to those who could take them !

A Highland army going into battle must have

been a terrifying sight. Here, as on other fields, the claymores advanced so quickly that the cavalry were put to it to keep pace with them. And the blades bit deep, giving no quarter.

Some onlookers who watched the battle from a hill-top remarked a band of red-coats surrounded by clansmen. From their eminence it resembled a red diamond with a dark struggling border. Gradually the diamond became smaller, until not one soldier was left alive.

Amongst those killed in the Highland troops were the Chief of Clan Ranald and the Earl of Strathmore.

Scott recounts that when the Clan Ranald men saw their chief fall mortally wounded, they were inclined to waver until Glengarry rushed forward crying: " Revenge—to-day for vengeance—to-morrow for mourning!"

You may slay men like those—but you cannot subdue them !

Still the heather grows and a clean wind blows over the moor where men fought and died, many, perhaps, never really knowing why, and through the pines the sighing of the breeze is unceasing coronach for those men who died well.

A few yards, and I came upon a cairn—erected by the Clan Macrae exactly two hundred years after the Battle of Sheriffmuir to witness and speak of the deeds their tartan had accomplished !

It was erected to the memory of the Kintail and Lochalsh companies of the clan, who formed part of the left wing of the Jacobite army and fell almost to a man.

A solitary cyclist was leaning against the stone dyke, anxious to know if I had seen his friends. He did not know much about the place, but hazarded the view that the " gathering stone " was somewhere up the path on the right.

It was almost dark now, but I wanted to see one stone—anything at all rather than home unappeased, and so I climbed the dyke and kept along the dank wet path.

There may be a stone there—indeed there is little doubt there is, but I have not seen it. Squelching through heather holes, amongst recumbent wire, over a burn with soft, treacherous banks in the half-dark, and always in front more heather-clad wastes.

The stone eluded me. The moon came up, white and beautiful, the hills were suddenly bathed in silver, and the scene was one I shall never forget, but through it all I had a pang in my heart. The stones had eluded me in a land I want to know and take to my heart ; I had ventured my last free day amongst the age-old traditions of this wonderful westland, and in giving my last I had lost.

XIV

GLENARTNEY

Come when the moon is high
And see the reivers' ghosts go by !

Many times have I passed through Crieff on my way north, and the clean attractive little town always held its appeal. It is a delightful place to explore, full of romance and tales of other days, with a literary flavour too, as here was born David Mallet who, with James Thomson, wrote "Alfred," in which appeared "Rule Britannia," while not far from the town is laid the scene of Ian M'Laren's "Drumtochty," but the world of to-day, forgetting the "kailyard school," in its reading shows a preference for stronger meat. But this morning I had no time to loiter—a long day was in front, a long road to traverse.

The "Highland Line" runs through the town, so that it stands, as it were, a buttress between Highland and Lowland, and for many years was the centre of a great cattle Tryst when the dwellers of the hills brought down their black cattle, and buyers from the lowlands and even south of the border attended in great numbers. Tumultuous scenes were sometimes enacted, the men of the North, proud, haughty and quick of temper, and the lowlander—who had not been by then altogether tamed and softened by law and custom—equally ready to hold his own. Indeed the gallows—" the kind Gallows of Crieff "—was never long without its hideous ornaments. Law-giving was strict here, as it had to be ! The town lay too close to the wild hills and glens to run undue risks, and self-preservation demanded a strong hand when dealing with marauding or quick-handed gentry.

Sir Walter Scott mentions a quaint custom amongst the Highland drovers who, when passing the gallows on their way to or from the town, used to touch their bonnets and mutter, " God bless her nainsel, and the Tiel tamn you."

Whatever indignities or stringent laws Crieff forced on the clansmen, they got it all back with full measure when, in 1715, they burned the town and practically wiped it out. A like fate was narrowly averted when the army of Bonnie Prince Charlie were retreating from Stirling in the '45, but better councils prevailed.

Heart-rending as were the scenes when the whole populace were left without a shelter to their heads, many with hardly a rag to cover them, the new town which gradually sprang from the ashes of the old is certainly a most delectable spot, and forms a delightful starting-point from which to " plunge into that most paradisaical part of all the paradise of Strathearn, the seven miles between Crieff and Comrie," as Chambers has it !

To-day there was no sign of anything but peace and goodwill as I came down the hilly streets bathed in glorious sunshine, but in a moment the hills had me in their grip again !

Far on the left, high above the intervening trees,

stood the Baird Monument, as if to guard wild
Glenartney and its dark secrets.

It's a roundabout way the road out of Crieff
by the west, as if half-hearted about crossing the
Highland line, and anxious to delay the adventure
as long as possible! And certainly the hills look
daunting enough—wild and menacing, indeed, in
their frowning strength.

Over the Turret water, crooning away to itself
as if singing the praises of the scenic beauties it
had passed on its journey through the hidden glens
beyond.

The road dips, and in a moment the hills are
gone—everything is lowland and domestic, an anti-
climax to the view of a hundred yards back. But
only for a moment, and soon again the hills and
pine-clad slopes dominate the view, their stern
beauty softened by a plenitude of silver birch; an
added grace to the rugged outlook.

The road was good, the sun genial and warm, a
lark was trilling, and on every side were bowers of
trees flanked by hills. Truly it was a fine start for
a day which bade well and fair.

And then on my right appeared a vista of lake
and wood so compelling in its beauty that my
measured miles were forgotten, and for long I
lingered. A swan was gliding on the calm surface
of the lake, and its reflection in the water, this
perfect morning, added a quaint touch to the scene.
No matter how often or at which season, Ochtertyre can never be passed by anyone who seeks
perfection in landscape.

Here Robert Burns visited Sir William Murray

and saw beauty which, in his eyes, even surpassed
that of Nature, in the person of Miss Euphemia
Murray of Lintrose, the niece of his host. A girl
of eighteen, she was already known as " The Flower
of Strathmore," and the poet in his tribute to her
charms bestowed upon her undying fame.

> Blythe, blythe, and merry was she,
> Blythe was she but and ben ;
> Blythe by the banks of Earn,
> And blythe in Glenturit glen.
>
> The Highland hills I've wander'd wide,
> And o'er the lawlands I hae been ;
> But Phemie was the blythest lass,
> That ever trode the dewy green.

Miss Murray afterwards became the wife of a
Court of Session Judge, and was doubtless forgotten
by the bard, whose wandering fancy created so many
immortals.

Not the least picturesque feature hereabouts are
the wonderful old beeches, and I found myself
wondering if Burns had passed beneath their
spreading branches in days long gone by.

The hedgerow bank was equally beautiful if in a
less conspicuous manner, a perfect carpet of hartstongue ferns with here and there a nestling straw-
berry plant. The little starry flowers which earlier
had lent an extra feature to the greenery had by
now given place to the delicate miniature fruit so
neglected because of its modest self-effacement, but
too luscious and sweet to be ignored.

The road was a succession of winding bends,
each in turn adding a new beauty to the view.

In a field I surprised a gathering of rooks, a parliament in session, only there was no official speaker. Even had there been, every individual was too busy airing his own views to pay much attention to rules of debate.

There were hundreds of them, possibly thousands, at least the whole field was glossy with their black coats.

A car passed, and the sable cohorts rose into the air and circled and gyrated in a most bewildering manner ere settling down again to discuss the obviously weighty problems which had convened the meeting.

For a mile or two the dominant note on the landscape had been the tall commanding pillar of the Baird Monument, occupying a high wooded eminence. Somehow it reminded me of Cleopatra's Needle as it stood, dark and straight, overtopping the attendant trees ; I found later, when standing alongside, that it was built of granite, almost white, and sparkling in the sun.

Soon I was climbing the narrow winding path to the summit, an effort well worth the labour and bringing an abundant reward.

Underfoot was dark and moss-grown, and so rarely is the pathway frequented that on several occasions I had to brush aside the overhanging branches or literally break through rank under-growth. The very birds seemed to resent my intrusion, and every now and then a blackbird— self-appointed guardian of the country-side—gave hurried warning of my approach.

From time to time I passed huge iron rings

attached to great sunken blocks, presumably used in hauling up the mighty stones of which the monument is built. Some of the stones which form the base appeared to my inexperienced eye to weigh many tons, and it must have been a Herculean task getting them to the summit of the steep, broken hill-side.

From the top, where the trees allow, the view is magnificent—Crieff below looking in the rarefied atmosphere like a model town built by some lad.

Robert Chambers tells us that " seen from the south Crieff looks like a troop of men hurrying up out of the low country into the Highlands," but I could not get that aspect of it, although, of course, the Crieff of to-day must be a vastly different place from that which he knew.

The monument, you may know, was erected to Sir David Baird, hero of Seringapatam. The original edifice was struck by lightning some forty odd years ago, and almost destroyed, but it was rebuilt—and an imposing landmark it is !

This hill on which it stands is named Tom-a-chastel, and age-old tradition states that at one time a castle occupied the site, and an admirable vantage-point it must have been. The Royal Castle of Earne, no less, and for her part in a conspiracy against Robert the Bruce, the Countess of Strathearn was doomed to perpetual imprisonment in the dungeon.

The vegetation on the hill or mound is luxuriant, indeed the red campion still lingered although by now a mere memory of the hedgeside in most places.

THE OLD BRIDGE, STIRLING

Apart from the soft rustle of leaves, there was a Sabbath quiet over the place. The cooling breeze was welcome, and the world of to-day seemed very far away as I sat down on the grassy bank and filled my pipe.

The view commanded every airt—and every quarter has its story. Down there where the highway runs, to-day so peaceful as to be almost lonely in its aspect, was enacted long ago one of those fierce lawless affairs so intermixed with the story of our land.

This is Murray country, and that family had long been at feud with their neighbours, the Drummonds, and on this occasion would appear to have been the aggressors.

As fancy took them, the Murrays from time to time harried the Drummond lands and carried off spoil and cattle, doubtless with counter reprisals on the part of the Drummonds, and so things went on, just as was happening in many other parts of the land, between warring factions. These were mere raids and excursions, and, considering the times, not really serious !

Ultimately the rival clans met in pitched battle, and the Drummonds were defeated.

The victors had gone off with the spoils of war once again, when Campbell of Dunstaffnage, with a large body of his clansmen, arrived on the scene.

Dunstaffnage had come on a mission of vengeance on the Murrays, as that clan had murdered his father-in-law, and so joining forces with the defeated Drummonds, instantly followed the Murrays into their stronghold.

N

With the odds now heavily against them, and fatigued by their recent battle exertions, the Murrays, with their wives and children, took refuge in the church of Monzievaird.

This sanctuary was unknown to their enemies, and might have remained undiscovered had not a Drummond, on passing near-by the place of concealment, so incited one of the hidden Murrays that, unable to restrain his passion, he seized a bow and shot the man from a window.

Now, of course, the secret was out, and the church immediately surrounded. The Murrays were called upon to surrender, but refused to do so.

The building, which was thatched with heather, was set alight, and the inmates, some hundred and sixty men, women and children, perished in the flames.

Sorrowful old memories these to hang over such a smiling country-side as this to-day, but many dark tales are associated with these same hills, and it was not always the deer or grouse that men hunted as quarry over the heather wastes or amongst the rocks.

Over there amongst the dark hills lies wild Glenartney, but it does not show to greatest advantage from this elevation. Indeed, it is a glen that takes some knowing—lonely, forbidding, almost unapproachable in its demeanour. Somehow to me it looks as if brooding over the past, regretful of the days when the royal house claimed its deer as a right; of its departed glories, when men strove for its possessions and nameless deeds found their stage in its bosom.

Down there on the plain of Lochlane, near-by Strowan House, Prince Charlie is said to have reviewed his troops ere retreating to the fatal North by way of the Sma' Glen. There is a local story, too, that Queen Anne spent some time at Lochlane House, so the place has many royal traditions.

To-day the glen proper is for the pedestrian only—its associations still immune from all who cannot woo it gently and unhurried. Unless you care for solitude, for the free wind which blows from the hills, keep to the King's highway—the glen's secrets are not for you !

But—if you love the tales of old: to dwell on the days when rival factions strove and no man was protected by other than his own right arm, when even the King's rights were flouted and the royal venison a perquisite of all who had the courage to take what they coveted—if that you love, then here you will find a plenty !

The glen will always be associated with an atrocious deed of blood, the onus of which is, rightly or wrongly, laid at the door of the MacGregors. There may be a doubt about the actual perpetrators of the act—one of the blackest in Highland blood feud, not because of the actual deed but for the incidents which clothed it ; but as the MacGregors have many gruesome outrages placed to their record, their shoulders are broad enough to carry this one also, although the Glencoe Macdonalds may not be altogether innocent. The Privy Council, at least, had no hesitation in placing the crime to the Clan Gregor !

The tale goes that the King—James VI—had

his deer-forest in Glenartney, and, to celebrate his nuptial feast, instructions were issued to Drummond-Ernoch, the warden of these hills, to secure a supply of venison for the royal table.

When about his lawful business in the deer-forest, Drummond-Ernoch and his men came upon a band of MacGregors helping themselves to the royal venison.

The King's forester executed summary punishment on the outlaws by cropping their ears as a warning that the royal estates must be free of such vagrants, and then let them go.

Better for him had his work been more complete, as ere long the MacGregors were on his track, roused to their very depths at the insult put upon their tartan and bitter for vengeance.

Soon their chance came, and one day, meeting Drummond-Ernoch in Glenartney, they slew him and cut off his head, which, wrapped in a plaid, they took along with them as proof of their bloody work.

On their way home by Loch Earn, they passed the old mansion-house of Ardvorlich, and reading by the signs that the men-folk were absent on some business of their own, they entered the house and demanded food.

The lady of the house, a sister of the slain Drummond-Ernoch, knowing there was blood feud between them, was glad to get off so easily. At once she placed bread and cheese before the Mac-Gregors, saying that this might stay their pangs until she prepared something more substantial.

One of the uninvited guests demanded a cup of

water, and when she returned from the well, there on the table, the mouth stuffed with bread and cheese, was the gory head of her brother !

With a shriek she fled from the house, and for some days wandered about the hill-sides like a mad woman. Ultimately she was found and brought home to Ardvorlich, where shortly she gave birth to a son, James Stewart, referred to elsewhere, who became notable for his physical strength and uncontrolled passions.

Meanwhile the MacGregors departed for their native glens, taking the ghastly trophy along with them.

On the following Sabbath the head of Drummond-Ernoch was laid on the altar of Balquhidder Church and the MacGregors, one by one, placed their hands on the head and swore to protect the perpetrators of the deed and share in the consequences, whatever they might be !

The Government took a very serious view of the business, and letters of fire and sword were issued against the clan. Neighbouring chiefs and lairds drove against the MacGregors, and much blood was spilt, and doubtless opportunity was seized to pay off many outstanding scores on either side.

There is an air of deep mystery about Glenartney, making it easy to weave romantic tales, and here many broken men have sought sanctuary in the days of reif, providing as it does easy escape to the western hills and seas.

James IV spent some happy days " a-chasing the deer " in Glenartney, and unlike the modern stalker, who will spend fruitless hours on the hill only to find his wary quarry too alert and elusive and the heavy trail vain, he went forth with all the panoply of majesty. Surrounded by nobles and courtiers, with numerous ghillies and attendants, a goodly company and a brave, they doubtless accomplished considerable execution amongst the native royalty of the glen.

A minor fight, but serious enough in its own way, took place in the glen one October evening in the days of Rob Roy.

The MacGregors were the aggressors, and having *lifted* a huge drove of cattle, they were making for home when they were overtaken by the irate owners. The ensuing battle was a brisk enough affair, the pursuers determined to recover their property, the reivers just as stubborn to retain their ill-gotten spoil, and a number of men paid the penalty ere the issue was decided in favour of the rightful owners. Farming or cattle-breeding was a business fraught with considerable risk near-by the Highland Line !

Fights and skirmishes amongst wild clansmen—desperate sallies after the protected deer make good reading, and moreover one can fully understand them because of the times—but the cloud of a darker tragedy hangs over the glen—one which even now it is hard to forgive.

Indeed one of the most vindictive deeds ever committed by a Government was the arrest and execution of Dr Archibald Cameron, brother of Lochiel, in 1753, for the part he had played in the rising under Prince Charles Edward Stuart. It is true that he was specifically mentioned in the Act of Attainder of high treason, but by the date of his arrest the country was sick of the butchery which followed Culloden.

Lochiel having died in France, Dr Cameron is thought to have been actuated by a desire to offer advice and assistance to his fatherless nephews, so he returned to his native land and spent some time in hiding in Glenartney.

How his presence in the West was conveyed to the Government is not now material, although there is a strong suspicion that some spy, afraid that Dr Cameron was home to make inquiry as to the whereabouts of a large sum of money, remitted by the French Government to aid the clans in their insurrection, and which had mysteriously disappeared, did so to protect himself.

Be that as it may, a party of soldiers from the garrison at Inversnaid, advised of his whereabouts, effected his arrest, and he was at once sent under escort to Stirling. From there he was transferred to Edinburgh and then to the Tower of London.

He was put on trial in May, and although seven years of exile had intervened, the court found him guilty and he was sentenced to death.

One favour only was granted—the execution date was put forward by a week to enable his wife to return from Flanders and see him for the last time.

When lying under sentence, the use of pens and paper was refused, but Cameron secured some stray scraps of paper and wrote some pencil notes for his wife recounting some of the occasions on which he had been enabled during the rising to prevent reprisals and save much bloodshed. One of these deeds was when, by his personal exertions, he prevented the whole town of Kirkintilloch from being given to the flames and the inhabitants put to the sword.

It is a commentary on the barbarous Government of the day that Dr Cameron was conveyed to Tyburn, suspended for some twenty minutes, when he was taken down, his head cut off, his heart torn out, and burnt !

Fear and sycophancy made cowardly judges !

Back to the main road again, I set my face towards Comrie—a road which could tell of strange untoward happenings ere it became a public highway free to all.

Montrose lay one night at Crieff almost three hundred years ago, and must have retreated this way before the superior forces of Baillie, who had marched against him from Perth in the hope of a daybreak surprise.

But Montrose was too good a soldier, too experienced a tactician to be caught napping. Outnumbered by horse and foot, he made his way along the Earn to Comrie, crossed the stream and went by way of Ardvorlich's lands to Lochearnhead. Next day the Highlanders marched to Balquhidder, where Montrose was joined by Lord Aboyne, and doubtless more than one fighting man of Clan Gregor found the warlike Montrose too fascinating to resist and threw in his lot with that gallant leader, to do his part, a month later, in Auldearn, never again perhaps to see his native braes.

Still winding in its leisurely way, but now tree-lined, the leafy branches meeting overhead, the road was restful and enchanting.

The massive pile of Lawers House, seat of an old Scottish family, is a notable feature on the landscape.

Some two hundred years ago the cloud of tragedy was cast over this stately old home. Sir James Campbell of Lawers had a close friend and confidant, one Duncan Campbell of Edramurkle. Sir James and this false companion had gone to visit a young lady to whom the former was shortly to be married. On their way home they spent a day or two together in Greenock, and being short of cash but anxious to buy a pistol when in a town, Edramurkle borrowed a sum from his trusting friend of Lawers.

That night, when Sir James was fast asleep, Edramurkle requited his kindness by shooting him twice through the head, and absconding before the deed was discovered. Robbery was said to be the motive, and although the—in those days—large reward of one hundred guineas was offered for information which would lead to the arrest of the murderer, I do not think he was ever brought to trial.

Soon now I passed over the bridge which spans the Lednock Water and entered the quiet little town of Comrie.

Samson, as we know, amused himself by tossing a huge boulder about on Ben Ledi's side, indeed all the world knows, because the stone as proof still lies where he threw it, to the wonder of all lesser mortals. But Callander had not a monopoly of these exuberant displays of thew and sinew. Here, too, Samson visited in his wanderings, and by way of physical exercise, or maybe only from mere joy of living, he flung some huge stones from the neighbouring hills, and later those mysterious Druids made use of them for their pagan rites.

Comrie appears to have spent its early years under rather trying circumstances. If it is true that Galgacus and Agricola fought their great battle here, other notable occurrences must appear as mere incidents, but the series of earthquakes which it has undergone lend it an unchancy reputation.

To-day it is a smiling, sunlit town, benign and happy-looking, as if it at least found the modern world treating it well, and was endeavouring to atone for its somewhat noisy past.

No one should pass Comrie without climbing the hill road and viewing the Devil's Cauldron—a sight well worth the exertion, even if it does " gie ye a pech," as an old man predicted when first I ventured there.

Up you go—up until you wonder if the labour entailed is worth while—but it always is on these hill-roads, and the clear free air is a tonic and a delight.

I have traversed this road in all weathers—when wind was blowing and whistling down the glens— rain lashing and biting, and mist enveloping the hills like angry smoke. Again when all was white beneath a mantle of deep snow and the bens stood out with an added beauty. Then you can trace the hare and the fox. Here a rabbit made its useless effort to escape the feral weasel : under there you know some game birds slept—the shepherd's footprints are clear—the spot where he stopped to examine something and his collie circled round. It is all there clear to the discerning eye —the story of the wild told by their loitering or hurrying feet.

Climb up some day and see it for yourself—the carpet of hartstongue ferns, the tormented battling water—these alone will fill your eye with a beauty you are not likely to forget.

From Comrie to St Fillans is the most beautiful part of the road. On the left for quite a stretch a guard of pine, fir and larch—green all the year round and fitting into their setting most admirably, while on the right heavy dark hills, broken and rugged.

A mile or so, and the Earn comes close to the roadside and sings a cheery chorus to the wayfarer. Across the railway and opposite a conical hill, which always appears to remain green no matter how its neighbours change their shades, is a sight to instil terror to the more timid. This is a wild-looking monster rushing down the hill-side, huge fangs gleaming, withal a frenzied-looking creature.

In truth it is merely a stone, carved by nature into the form of a huge crocodile, and a paint-pot in an idle hand has completed the likeness. It is "tethered" to the hill-side by a rope, and legend states that the monster has been chained up in this way since one memorable New Year morning when it chased Rob Roy across the hills !

And then St Fillans. With the evening sun

glinting on the loch, every cottage embowered in blossom, the shadow of Ben Vorlich almost at its feet, it would be difficult to choose a more delightful halting-place. Over there where the Neishes paid such a dire penalty to the outraged Macnabs, a man and a girl were fishing in the cool of the evening, an occasional plop and the widening rings on the placid loch sure proof that a cunning hand need not lack sport enough and to spare. And then the sun went down behind the hills in a wonderful glory of colour, and but for an occasional mysterious woodland sound from the other side of the loch, the world seemed asleep.

XV

OVER THE REST TO INVERARAY, LOCH FYNE AND THE CAMPBELL COUNTRY

Over the hills to the setting sun,
  (Hark to the song of the burn)
By the cloud-kissed ben and the winding glen,
  (A road that your heart will travel again)
And the peace that your heart will earn.

THE road to the Campbell country is well guarded. If you go by Loch Long-side the deep sea loch is there as a foil, and if your way lie from Tarbet as did mine this day, the old Cobbler stands sentinel, keeping a weather-beaten eye on you as if ready to flash the tidings from his lofty perch far across the intervening hills to the watch-tower on Duniquaich Hill guarding the clanship in Inveraray.

Once through Arrochar and round the top of Loch Long you cross the narrow bridge which spans the burn, " the brown grey river," as it is named, past Ardgarten, and then you are fairly on the highway to adventure, mist and mountains.

The *highway* to adventure is a proper term, because almost before you realise it Rest-and-be-thankful has you in her toils, and you are mounting up and up with no seeming respite until the very mountain caps appear to await your coming. The

Rest, as they call it for short, is a long pull and a sore.

Almost at the summit there is a hairpin bend which haunts the nervous motorist, and if now no great ordeal to the modern high-power car, it is not exactly the sort of place one wants to chance every day.

As always in these parts we are in the wake of armed forces. Long before Bruce climbed up this rugged path it was a battle-ground for King Arthur away back in the sixth century, and was doubtless the scene of many an ambush and foray down the intervening years.

The Dutchmen are said to have had a camp on Loch Long and to have brought wine here to trade with the Highlanders; and generations ago, as we know, the Norsemen harried and laid waste its shores with fire and sword.

If it no longer echoes to the slogan of the clansman or the fierce shouts of the invaders, this morning I had an experience exciting enough of its kind. Two-thirds up and going strong ere changing down to negotiate the bend, a flock of sheep spilled round the corner and came slowly down the hill to meet me.

It is not a nice place to stop at any time, but to jam on brakes and hold up until the baaing creatures meandered past was more than I had bargained for. Behind them the shepherd was beckoning me to come on, and then I sensed, rather than heard, his whistle. Two dogs seemed to spring from nowhere, and the sheep were off the road and on the hill-side in less time than it takes to write the words, and with a shouted, but I fear unheard, thanks, I was safely round the bend and at the summit.

Here stands a stone admonishing all travellers to " Rest and be thankful," and filling a pipe I stood on a rock and followed with my eyes my shepherd and his flock, now far below. It is only from this vantage with the long winding road and far valley that one fully realises what a climb this is, or how :

> Now wound the path its dizzy ledge,
> Around a precipice's edge.

Once again my soul is filled with admiration for old General Wade, the wonder-worker, for this, too, is part of his living handiwork. " The incontro-vertible general," Robert Chambers styled him for his manner of making roads " as straight as his per-son, as undeviating as his mind, and as indifferent to steep braes as he himself was to difficulties in the execution of his duty "—surely an epitaph eulogistic enough for any man, yet one richly deserved.

There is a strange fascination in standing on some high, wind-swept place, and here the glorious white-capped hills behind, dark Loch Restal in front, the far-winding descent and the deep glen form a pic-ture not likely to fade from the mind.

On the way up to this vantage spot dark Glencroe is apt to be missed by the man at the wheel, but to appreciate its fearsome beauty one should do it on foot, as I have on many occasions, and then its lovely ruggedness is almost overawing. Whenever I find outstanding characteristics in the topography of my country, I always refer to Robert Chambers, that wonderful man whose every minute must have brought its task, so indefatigable was he in his writings.

Sure enough he had been here, and his description of Glencroe would stand to-day as then : no word need be altered, so perfect is his picture.

Let me quote him, and if you know the road, at once you will recognise how true he is : " In lonely magnificence, and all the attributes of Highland valley scenery, Glencroe can only be considered inferior to the vale which so nearly resembles its name. Its sides are covered with rude fragments of rock ; and a little stream runs wildly along the bottom, as if anxious to escape from its terrible solitudes."

The long, narrow road is now more track than highway, huge rocks and boulders strew the path, while right and left the mountain-sides reach up to meet the blue,

And heath-bells bud in deep Glencroe.

To-day there are no heath-bells, either here or in the glen which is now just behind, only withered bracken, and it appears lonely and desolate ; indeed, one almost awaits to hear a shout of " Cruachan " or "Loch Sloy" and to see the green tartan, or the red, bar the way, but only a whaup calls or a sheep bleats, for the clansmen warriors of other days are gone.

Leave the pathway for a little and one is almost lost to time. A well-known Glasgow man told me of his two young nieces who had fallen victims to the prevailing sun-bathing habit.

INVERARAY

One glorious summer evening, on passing through this glen, so quiet and travel-free was the road, they changed into their bright-hued bathing costumes.

On climbing the hill-side they started playing hide-and-seek among the rocks, when they espied an old shepherd coming slowly towards them. Full of pranks and high spirits, they danced gracefully towards the old man, when, to their astonishment, he stood for a moment terror-stricken and then turned and ran as for dear life !

Some lonely shieling would that night hear of the fairies he had seen on the mountain-side—who knows ?

Leaving " Rest and be thankful " we soon come to cross-roads, the first break in our journey. The quick turn on the left across the bridge goes by St Catherine's, through far Glen Branter to the Cowal shore, but our quest takes us to the right.

A beautiful road indeed, but for us a short, sharp descent requiring wary going, past Kilmorich Church, round by Cairndow Inn, and Loch Fyne bursts into view. There is a tang of sea-wrack and the clear, strong air is a tonic for jaded nerves like the fairy wind which blows from " Seven glens and seven bens and seven mountain moors," as no doubt it does and to spare.

Loch Fyne herrings have been a delicacy for many generations of gourmets. Long ago the Frenchmen used to steer their barques here and exchange ankers of wine for the fish, and so valuable was the traffic that the name Loch Fyne was derived from the French rendering of " the loch of wine."

o

A beautiful countryside this — hill - encircled, wooded, yet open to the sea, what more suitable environment for the great MacCailein and his Campbell henchmen ?

If it appears calm and tranquil to-day it was not always so, and most of the neighbouring clans were ready—not, perhaps, without due cause—to drop their hunting or pastoral pursuits and take up the claymore against these Argyllshire men.

The history of our country is full of references to Argyll and the Campbell Clan, but their real story will never be written, and perhaps it is well that much should be forgotten.

Many travellers have followed this beautiful lochside road we are traversing to-day, but there is one whose story interests me particularly.

Nearly two hundred years ago—in the year 1751 —two fair beauties burst upon London " and turned the West End almost mad." They were sisters, " the two fair Gunnings," as they were called, and on one occasion there was an unprecedented scene at a Court drawing-room, the gentlemen present climbing upon chairs and tables to look at them. In any case, the Duke of Argyll married the elder when she was left a widow by the Duke of Hamilton, and as she had two sons by each of her ducal husbands she was thus wife of two Dukes and mother of four !

If she came this road which to-day is ours alone, driving in her heavy coach across the bridge at the loch head, with its fragrant pine woods, in summer days heavy with the scent of honeysuckle, I wonder, sophisticated as she must have been, what were her thoughts when she turned her back on it all once more to seek the far-away London Court ?

Soon, too soon, so wondrous is the Highland roadway, we are passing Inveraray Castle, home of the Argylls, and the little town is upon us.

It has changed its position now, for in the old days the houses clustered near the Chief's ducal home, but as it is, the setting is perfect, and a trim and beautiful little township it is.

When Burns visited Inveraray, the inn was full to overflowing, guests and retainers of the Duke occupying every available corner, and in the hubbub and excitement the poet was ignored and slighted, and gave vent to his feelings in a bitter verse :

> There's nothing here but Highland pride,
>   And Highland cauld and hunger ;
> If Providence has sent me here,
>   'Twas surely in His anger.

Perhaps, however, he who knew so much of Scottish life and character was prejudiced against the Loch Fyne people, for many a tale would he hear of their ruthless methods when an overweight of numbers gave them security. Burns had a wonderful admiration for Glencairn, and mayhap knew of how an ancestor of the Earl he so revered was tricked and deserted in his hour of need by an Argyll and his clansmen.

The occasion was that known in Scottish history as Glencairn's Expedition to the Highlands, and this army, commanded by the Cunningham chief, who had with him Lochiel, Atholl, Glengarry, Graham of Duchray, MacGregor, and several others, was joined by Argyll with one thousand foot and some fifty horse. Argyll had apparently become faint-hearted and decided to withdraw with all his personal forces.

Glencairn despatched Lochiel and Glengarry to compel the Campbells to return to their positions, and they were overtaken somewhere in the vicinity of Castle Ruthven, then in the hands of the English, but Argyll escaped with a remnant of his mounted retainers.

The Campbell clansmen, thus deserted by their leader, offered to return and again join issue with Glencairn, but Glengarry would have none of it, and was on the point of attacking them when the timely arrival of his general, Glencairn, prevented what would doubtless have been a massacre.

They were ordered to lay down their arms before any treaty could be entertained, and on their declared willingness again to take the field and loyally stand by their leader, they were bound by oath to keep word and faith. All ranks subscribed —and within a fortnight every single man among them had deserted ! The Glencairn rising was ultimately quelled by General Monk, and several of the officers were hanged.

But that is an old story now, and to-day Inveraray was a-bustle with men and beasts ; for there was a cattle sale on hand ; most interesting, not to say exciting, affairs were in progress.

The green in front of the hotel was fenced in to form one huge enclosure, and as droves of shaggy, wild-eyed cattle or flocks of sheep and rams arrived, they were driven into this common arena to mix indiscriminately.

Many a fierce combat was being waged by the young bulls. Now and again a sharp clap told of two rams " hurtling " at each other, while all unconcerned, groups or odd couples of shepherds, farmers, and drovers stood smoking and chatting, awaiting the all-important personality, the auctioneer, now and again administering an admonitory whack on a too bold or inquisitive animal.

It was like a scene from another country. Gaelic was the speech, the gentry in their Campbell tartans, while in the midst stood the beautiful war memorial to the Lochfyneside lads who would know it no more.

I do not know how old Inveraray is in the annals of men, but Bruce fought here; but an older memory than even that of the Bruce adorns the place in the form of a stone cross, said to have been removed from Iona.

Apart from the short summer season when tourists pay fleeting visits, they live in a world of their own in this Campbell quarter. Easily enough got at to-day, perhaps, but it is interesting to note that in 1691 an Act was passed by the Convention of Royal Burghs exempting Inveraray from certain taxes because of the difficulty of access to the place !

Gilpin, the Prebendary of Salisbury, toured Scotland in the closing years of the eighteenth century and left an interesting record of much that he saw.

Amongst other places, his wanderings took him to Inveraray, and he records that at certain seasons the natives declare Loch Fyne to be one part water and two parts herring! In one bay of the loch there were sometimes to be seen six hundred boats engaged in fishing.

He relates that amongst the implements on board each boat the bagpipes were rarely forgotten, and the "shrill melody" could be heard resounding from every part.

On Sunday evenings the crews put away their bagpipes and the shore echoed to their singing of Psalms!

But more stirring deeds have found their setting here in the days when might was right and a chief's word law.

To me, the seventeenth century holds a rare fascination.

In many aspects it marked the parting of the ways.

If manners were uncouth, bloodshed not by any means uncommon, torture and horrible sentences meted out by the law, nevertheless the right hand was groping towards culture and the arts while the left still firmly held to mere savagery.

It is true the peasant of the Lowlands was illiterate and credulous; the clansman of the North barbaric, and asked for nothing other than to carry out the will of his chief—but a new spirit was abroad.

The clergy, coarse and outspoken as they may now appear, were leading, blindly it may have been, to a spiritual freedom which was ultimately to spell emancipation for the whole land. Many of the Highland chiefs were, even if only in trust, great landowners. Several of them acquainted with courts, sending their sons into the outer world to be educated, were yet cruel and high-handed.

In a century which recognised Shakespeare, Courts of Justice were a misnomer, and in Scotland more often than not the colour of a man's tartan did more to condemn him than the deeds for which he was arraigned.

On a spring evening in the year 1671, a number of Highland gentlemen met in Inveraray in the house of a certain John Rowat. Why they were assembled there, what they were plotting or discussing I do not know, but the sequel proves them to have been an ill-assorted fellowship.

Apparently differences had arisen, the exchanges were heated, *and the candle having gone out*, some one shot the Laird of Lochnell, a near kinsman to the Duke of Argyll. A dangerous position for all concerned !

Argyll was not the man to allow this to pass, and although one Duncan MacGregor admitted that he had fired the fatal pistol, James Menzies of Culdares was imprisoned and charged with the crime.

To be tried in Inveraray before a Campbell jury for the murder of one sib to their clan allowed of only one verdict. Menzies contrived to petition the Privy Council to be allowed to " thole his assize " in Edinburgh, and Argyll was ordered to appear before that body to show reason why the prayer should not be granted.

I do not know the result, or what action was taken—influence rather than justice or charity would doubtless be the deciding factor—but my point is to emphasise the autocratic power, the eagerness to grasp every opportunity to pay off old scores, to avenge past clan wrongs even on an innocent man!

This incident is not an isolated one, nor was it peculiar to one territorial magnate or chief, but was unhappily too frequently a recognised procedure, as one finds if the annals of the times are sifted.

One of Scotland's historic mysteries is intimately connected with this town and is known as " the Appin murder." The tale has been told many times, and is part of our Scottish lore to-day.

In the days of the '45 the Campbells took the Hanoverian side, while the Stewarts of Appin were " out " with the Prince. The Stewart estates were, as a result, forfeited to the Crown, and Campbell of Glenure was entrusted with them.

One day, as Campbell was returning from Fort William, a shot rang out on the hill-side, and he dropped mortally wounded.

One James Stewart was arrested, taken to Inveraray, tried before a Campbell jury, and hanged for a murder he probably did not commit. Indeed, the secret of who actually fired the shot was well guarded, but there is little doubt, indeed, that an innocent man was made to suffer.

R. L. Stevenson has made the tale his own, and there you can read it for yourself.

Many tales are told, but of all the romances woven round this old Gaelic stronghold give me Neil Munro's " John Splendid." He has written more than one book centred round Inveraray, but no other haunts my memory like that fascinating romance.

Up one of these Inveraray streets rode John Splendid without a turn of the head—and left me wishing that I could hear more about him, where he disported his gallant figure, and what strange adventures befell him on the road.

I wonder which way he turned—if he came round the loch side by Cairndow and the road we have just left, or if he struck out toward the setting sun in the direction of Loch Awe.

All stories of this district enthral; many of them may not be true, but they fit their setting and the wild blood of the days that are gone.

Montrose harried the Campbell country in December 1644. For leadership and valour this campaign must take high rank. The passes, difficult at any time, were snowbound and almost impassable, but the spirit of feud and hate, combined with indomitable pluck, accomplished the seeming impossible.

The invaders swept across Argyll and spared no man fit to carry arms, putting all to the sword, burning, ravaging and houghing or driving the cattle before them. Villages, farmhouses, cottages, all were given to the flames, and Inveraray was sacked. Montrose then retired north and in the following January, at Inverlochy, surprised and routed an army four times his strength.

The Campbells fought with great courage, but their defeat was decisive. Argyll watched the fight from his galley, when his presence as an active leader might have been more useful to his men.

Time has softened much of the old clan feeling, but it is not yet dead. Men are not so open in their loves and hates to-day, but now and again the old fires spring to life, splutter for a little, and die out again.

Only a year or two ago a most spirited encounter took place between the Duke of Argyll and the parish minister of Inverchaolain over a font missing from Cairndow Church. There was a lengthy and bitter correspondence between them, and the Duke of Argyll dated one of his letters " On the Feast of St Patrick the Apostle, 1925," while the minister headed his reply, " On or about the Anniversary of the Lamont Murders, 1925," this being in reference to a massacre of the Lamonts by the Campbells on the Cowal shore, on which occasion, I think, the Provost of Dunoon was hanged for passing a too free criticism on the deeds then committed.

It's an old story now, but clan feelings die hard, and even in this year of grace I know otherwise peaceful citizens who can work themselves into a mild passion over wrongs committed many generations ago.

The Campbells were not always on the losing side, however. They were a great and powerful fighting clan, capable of putting many warriors in the field, and loyal to their chief.

They suffered much in the old lawless days, but Argyll was powerful in the councils of the nation and generally managed to protect his people in the raids and counter-raids which were a feature of the times.

They were ruthless in their vengeance when opportunity gave them power, but in that they were, mayhap, no worse than their neighbours.

a sprig of heather on its forelock, and everything was gay and colourful.

This morning the hard snow crunched beneath my tackets as I crossed the station yard, and a whistling errand-boy, a basket over his arm, was sliding on the path where the snow had been brushed clear.

Still it was fine to be back in Crianlarich again, high-lying and cold as it was to-day, indeed its elevated position is overlooked because of the towering bulk of Ben More and Stobinian. The wind was shrewd, but snow and wind were soon forgotten in the hearty welcome awaiting me.

At the hotel they predicted bad weather and heavy going—and they proved to be no false prophets, indeed it was altogether different from the joyous road I had so lately known, and in place of a kindly sun, above was a sky of slate-grey as if heavy with snow. Still, there was to be no turning back now, and a glance at two passing fishermen, one without an overcoat, renewed my waning faith.

The clan road of the old marauding days came up Glenfalloch and turned west shortly before the site of the Crianlarich we know, and so this morning it was on my left, but too deep in snow to give sign of its presence, although high on the overhanging bank where the old drove road led, stands the oldest house in the village.

At one time it was an inn, frequented by caterans and drovers, passing to or from the glens beyond, and was the scene of a tumultuous episode in the life of Rob Roy.

The Duke of Montrose, discovering that Rob Roy

and his men were living in the inn, and doubtless fearing this to be the preliminary to some lawless escapade, sent a party of his clansmen, in charge of a kinsman, Graham, and supported by some military, probably from Inversnaid, to capture the outlaw. Ascertaining that Rob Roy was sleeping in the inn and his clansmen were occupying a near-by barn, the Grahams attacked the inn at daybreak. But it is ill to catch a man like the MacGregor unprepared, and nothing daunted, Rob defended himself lustily.

Soon the noise brought the MacGregors to his assistance, but they were too heavily outnumbered to have any chance of success, and so Rob Roy made his escape through a back window, and he and his men got safely away to the wild braes above Loch Lomond, where they knew every rock and moss-hole and where pursuit was impracticable.

It was from Strathfillan that the MacGregors, making rendezvous with some other clans, made their warlike descent on Inveraray.

Tradition tells us that Macdonald of Glengarry had charge of this force, and that it numbered some fifteen hundred claymores.

One would have thought the Clan Gregor had enough excitement at their own doors without embarking upon further adventures of that kind, but they were ever a restless, fighting race, and about this period, 1715, the whole country was in a ferment due to Mar's Rising.

And now they were gaily embarking upon a further adventure aware that powerful enemies were plotting in their rear.

Just shortly before this Inveraray excursion, the MacGregors, numbering some seventy hardy warriors, landed on Inchmurrin, an island in Loch Lomond, used by the Duke of Montrose as a deer preserve.

When darkness fell, they again took to their boats and approached the village of Bonhill, hoping to surprise and plunder the place while the inhabitants were asleep.

Unfortunately for the marauders, their advance was discovered, and at once the alarm was given. The various kirk bells were set a-ringing and an urgent message despatched to the commander of Dumbarton Castle—only a mile or two distant.

That officer fired his guns as a sign that speedy aid was forthcoming, and foiled in their purpose, the MacGregors took to their boats and landed once more on the island of Inchmurrin. There they slaughtered a number of the deer and held a rude feast ere making for their native haunts at daybreak.

But they did not depart quite empty-handed. Every boat and craft on the lochside was their spoil, and they had quite a flotilla when at last they arrived at Inversnaid, having despoiled every owner on their way.

This was more than the authorities and the Lowland citizens could permit to pass unchallenged, and so an expedition was raised to punish the raiders. With so many boats in their possession no one was safe from annoyance and attack from the restless clansmen.

A strange and motley force went forth to punish the Rob Roy faction.

P

Paisley contributed some hundred and twenty volunteers. The Ayrshire towns of Kilmarnock, Ayr and Kilwinning sent roughly four hundred. This force sailed up Loch Lomond in man-o'-war boats from the fleet then lying in the Clyde, commanded by Naval officers, who had with them some three hundred bluejackets supported by some guns with their special crews.

Another force marched along the rough and difficult lochside, and it was comprised of men from Dumbarton, Cardross and the lower reaches of Loch Long. Campbell of Mamore, an uncle of the Duke of Argyll, followed in charge of a well-mounted party of gentlemen and retainers.

In due time this force reached their objective, Inversnaid. There lay the boats, one object of their quest, but no hostile band challenged their approach.

It was a beautiful October morning, the bracken turning from yellow to russet, the bens looking silently down on as motley a crew as had until then startled the deer on their broad shoulders—but of MacGregors there was no sign.

A few deserted turf-roofed huts were visible on the higher banks, but unguarded by their red-tartaned owners.

A shot from one of the guns carried away the roof of a cottage, and one or two old women scrambled through the low doorway and disappeared behind the hill as fast as their aged limbs could bear them, but still no defiant clansmen appeared to protect their heritage.

The forces were landed, and in martial array they

marched stiffly up the hill-path and formed up on the flat summit.

There they stood, drums beating, for some considerable time, but they had the place to themselves. Apart from one or two men who quietly watched them at too great a distance to be molested or interrogated, no living soul was apparently within miles of the intended battleground.

The next morning the gallant force sailed down the loch again, in their turn confiscating every boat they discovered on their journey, and once again the deer were left to browse in peace.

The going was not so bad as I had anticipated. The snow was hard and clean, and bus-tracks made a footpath easy to negotiate. Winding and narrow, round a bend and the village is lost, but now the hills close in on every side of the glen, and if only the sun had come out the picture would have been sublime in its grandeur.

High on the left is a flat stone—" The Place of Shouting" it is called in Gaelic—where a man could stand and give shouted warning of enemy approach from any position, so commanding is the site.

Black too against the brae lie the ruins of St Fillan's Chapel, with its old burial-ground and a more modern God's acre behind.

St Fillan holds high place amongst Scottish saints, and indeed it were meet that he did so, because his deeds were outstanding to a degree !

For a considerable time this sainted man lived in a monastery at Pittenweem, and when engaged in translating the Scriptures, his left hand gleamed so

in the darkness that he could carry on his work
without the aid of a lamp !

If all stories are true, Scotland owes much to this
venerable saint. At one time in the history of our
land, holy relics, pieces of the true Cross and so on,
were held in high esteem and worked many miracles
in their day, but St Fillan's legacy took the form of
winning a battle, and no inconsiderable event in
the annals of our race at that, indeed no less than
the glorious victory of Bannockburn !

King Robert the Bruce spent the evening previous
to that great clash of arms in devout contemplation
and intercession to God and St Fillan.

In the Bruce's tent reposed a silver case which
was supposed to contain a wonderful talisman,
forsooth an arm of the saint ! As the King was
engaged in his devotions, the case suddenly opened
and as mysteriously closed !

The chaplain who was with the Bruce and had
observed the untoward happening, immediately
approached the altar and, examining the casket,
cried out that a miracle had been performed.
Afraid lest the day might go against the Scots, and
fearful that the holy relic might fall into profane
hands, the chaplain had left the saint's arm behind
and only the empty casket graced the altar. The
sudden and unaccountable opening and closing of
the silver case had been to admit the arm, which
now reposed within !

The Bruce, realising the good omen, passed the
evening in pious devotions and thanksgiving—and
with what results on the morrow the whole world
is to-day familiar.

IN GLENORCHY, DALMALLY

TYPICAL ... ON THE ... [illegible]

About a mile farther on and close to the roadside is St Fillan's Holy Pool.

Here a quaint ceremony was at one time indulged in for the cure of lunatics. Part of the ritual was to tie securely the afflicted one and leave him lying on his back all night ! If in the morning the much-tried victim of such heroic measures was found freed of his bondage, the cure was adjudged to be successful and complete. If, on the contrary, the knots were too secure and in the morning he was still bound and helpless, he was considered to be still possessed—but what then took place, or what further measures were enacted, I personally cannot enlighten you.

The old church bell, used in the days of St Fillan, was called into operation during the mystic ceremonies, and for many years it lay open and unprotected upon a flat gravestone. There was a local belief that if anyone dared to lay covetous hands upon it the bell would, because of some unknown power potent within it, return to the spot of its own accord.

A passing Sassenach one day put its power to a practical test, and from that date the bell has not been seen!

But madmen were not the only victims of these dark waters. Witches, or rather those accused of being witches, were here subject to a test, and innocent or guilty, the poor wretches upon whom fell the evil eye of the witch-finder or about whose doings gossip got busy, had not much chance of escape. The milk of human kindness was a very sour commodity in those days, I am afraid.

In any case, the proceedings here were as effective as they were simple.

When an old woman was charged with being a witch she was taken to the Holy Pool, and her thumbs being bound together, she was then thrown into the water. If she at once sank and did not come up again she was adjudged innocent and her name freed from the odium of the charge; if she did not drown it was conclusive proof of her guilt, and she was fished out and burned! It was doubtless an interesting experiment to all concerned, with the possible exception of the poor old victims, and was at least delightfully simple in its method and procedure.

Across the white bridge—so named locally, not because of its colour—and under your feet is being enacted a transformation. The stream which flows under on the left is the Connernish, but when it comes out again on the right it has changed its title to the Fillan.

Just hereabouts on the left is what looks to be a pool or mountain tarn cupped amongst some rocks. But it is no pool, at least in name, and flourishes under the proud patronymic of Loch Righ, or the King's Loch.

Tradition derives the name from the fact that at the battle of Dalree, fought here, the Bruce's men, when retreating before the victorious M'Dougalls of Lorn, cast their weapons into the loch to aid their escape.

The smoke in front, rising in a huge grey spiral from amongst a guarding screen of trees, was Tyndrum, and as I drew nearer, on the hills behind

I could note the scars that show where a fortune went in an endeavour to establish lead-mines.

And now good fortune, in the guise of a Ford car, took me by the hand, and right glad was I to accept the proffered lift.

There was a decided change in the temperature, and the wind now had a vicious nip which boded ill for nightfall. A narrow burn, hidden deep in rocky sides, was now keeping us company on the right, and here and there huge icicles had formed. In places they had the semblance of a pipe-organ where they stood, or rather hung, in rows, six or seven feet in length and many thicker than a man's thigh.

The glen got narrower as we bumped along, and almost at the skirt of Ben Doran we left Perthshire behind and entered Argyll.

A wonderful panorama of hill and moor rich in tradition and romance is opening to the view. Argyll—the land of the strangers—has many tales to tell, and the casket of their setting is amongst the most beautiful of our land.

Stretched out in front lay a long white strath, and on the left a camp of wooden huts to house the army at work on the new Glencoe road which ran over on the left, removing hills or filling chasms as need arose. A wonderful feat of engineering, but the hundreds who will travel its macadamised surface towards dark Glencoe may possibly save much sweat, but they will miss the joyous adventure of the old road.

And then Glenorchy and her " proud mountains," an old-time fastness of the ill-fated Mac-Gregors, appeared majestic in her white garments on the left. Now starts the Black Mount, really a serried range of hills, their tenants Breadalbane's deer. Read *The High Tops of the Black Mount* by Lady Breadalbane if you would know more of its denizens.

Over behind these hills was the childhood home of Duncan Ban M'Intyre, but the cottage is now a mere heap of stones and the belling of the stags has displaced the laughter of children.

Up here on the Black Mount was staged another of these hot-blooded incidents with which the West is chequered.

Some MacGregors were hunting in the district, amongst them being the son of Glenstrae, and when seeking rest or refreshment in a house or inn they were joined by young Lamont on his way across the hills from Cowal on some business of his own.

The two young chieftains sat at meat together and everything seemed friendly and well. Later in the evening some discussion arose and the youths quarrelled. Hot-blooded and touchy, weapons were drawn and the MacGregor lay dead on the floor.

Here in the heart of the MacGregor country, unaccompanied as he was, Lamont's position was desperate, and he took to the hills with MacGregor's followers hot on his heels.

Knowing that escape was impossible, he fled in the direction of Glenstrae's stronghold, and out-distancing the avenging clansmen, he craved sanctuary from Glenstrae in person, father of the man he had slain.

Glenstrae, a generous, impulsive man, swore to

protect him, no matter what deed he had perpe-
trated. No sooner was he committed to his oath,
than the pursuing clansmen arrived, explained
what had taken place, and demanded that Lamont
be given over to feudal justice.

Glenstrae, shocked as he must have been at the
loss of his boy, refused to break his word and told
Lamont to have no fear, he was safe under that roof.

Next day, with a picked body of his clansmen,
Glenstrae personally escorted Lamont to the
borders of his own clan-territory. "Now," he
said on parting, "you are safely amongst your own
people and my pledge has been fulfilled. More I
cannot and will not do—but if you value your life
avoid my territory—keep clear of my clansmen—and
may Heaven forgive you for the sorrow you have
laid at my door."

Not long afterwards Glenstrae and his clan were
proscribed ; letters of fire and sword were given
against all who wore his tartan, and he was more
homeless than the deer in his corries or the eagle on
Ben Doran.

Then Lamont repaid Glenstrae in kind for his
generous deed, sheltered and protected him amongst
the wild hills of Cowal, and proved a friend to the
Clan Gregor when all men's hands were against
them !

Now over the high-arched bridge which spans
the Orchy and lends its name to the clachan, and
we bump and jolt alongside the stream, while far off
on the right the new road winds towards the sea.

Round the bend we go, bumping amongst the
ruts, sympathising with every agonised protest

from the springs, and Loch Tulla is spread in front, a vision of beauty compensating for the discomforts of the road. The fine old Scotch firs are said to be the lingering heirs of the Caledonian Forest, and one man informed me that when cutting peat he regularly came across giant roots, all that is now left of the great tree-covered tract where the wolf, and not man, was the deer hunter.

Rattling and bumping along over the snow-filled ruts, past the finely situated Shooting Lodge, and so to Inveroran Hotel, where I left my driver-host to continue on his lonely way over the appalling road (for a car) to Glencoe.

In the hotel a casual remark about a golden eagle which graced a corner of the room proved fruitful.

It has been a bad year for snow, and the great birds have been not uncommon in the district of late.

A shepherd coming home across the hills had the unwelcome attendance of a giant specimen for fully an hour. It fluttered—if one can use such an expression about a creature with a wing-spread of some six feet—above his head just out of reach of his crook, its wicked, cruel eyes on his dogs. He kept them close to heel, well knowing the fate of even a fighting collie once these great talons gripped it, and strong man as he is, was not sorry when, approaching his home, his unwelcome escort rose to a great height and was soon a mere speck in the northern sky.

Three splendid specimens have been seen of late more than once, and doubtless the lambs and hill-hares will be having an anxious time.

They told me too that a week or two ago some stalkers near Loch Awe came across a herd of deer running in frenzy with an eagle swooping above them, but on their approach it made off towards the Braemar hills.

After a day on the snow-covered hills, the genial heat of the fire played me a most unfriendly trick, or I might have gleaned some even more interesting facts from the company.

Later as I looked out on the dreary white stretch, the moon breaking through above, I thought of one who loved these hills well and of his word painting :

> The placid moon, the huge sky-cleaving Ben,
> The moor loch gleaming in the argent ray,
> The long white mist low-trailing up the glen,
> The hum of mighty waters far away.

If Professor Blackie's gifts as a poet are open to doubt, as is the fashion to-day with a certain school, his love for his country is never in question.

XVII

BY CRUACHAN AND LOCH AWE

Land of Campbells and MacDougalls,
    Where full many a practised hand,
Nerved with high heroic purpose,
    Poised the spear, and waved the brand.

PROFESSOR BLACKIE

In Glenorchy I had a stalker for company to-day, but his mind was too practical to give me any romantic details of the old days when the MacGregor tartan ruled the glen, though on salmon and deer his knowledge was encyclopædic.

Near here, he informed me, was fought one of those dour clan battles which to-day lend an added interest to the glens and straths. In far-off 1463 the Stewarts, aided by the MacLarens, fought a battle-royal with the MacDougalls, Campbells of Lorn and some MacFarlanes, but which side gained the victory, or what it was all about, he did not know.

When Dr Garnett, one of the old-time travellers, passed through Glenorchy, and indeed for many long years to follow, salmon could be had for the taking by any man who cared to exert himself. And so Dr Garnett witnessed a remarkable way of ensnaring the plentiful fish.

At Catnish a rock crossed the bed of the Orchy, reaching almost from side to side. The height of

THE PASS OF AWE

KILCHURN LOCH AWE

this natural dam was such that few salmon could leap over into the pool beyond. A basket was fixed transversely, and the baffled fish fell into the receptacle, and were lifted out at leisure.

The hills of the Black Mount towered above on the right; those of Auch guarded us on the left, but in their driven white they somehow appeared unreal, more resembling cloud effects than towering bens; but when the sun glinted on them for a moment or two, the whole vista was fairylike in its charm.

And then I was brought down to the hard realities of life. To me, at this point, the river took on an added beauty, rippling and shallow amongst a mass of rocks and stones. But to my companion its beauty was lost. "Waste-water," he termed it—no salmon were to be caught in such a stretch! So we tramped ahead, smoking our pipes and agreeing to differ about the real fundamentals of Highland glens.

Christopher North knew the Glenorchy region well, and used to perform wonderful feats of pedestrianism, impossible for the normal man to emulate.

Francis Watt tells how on one occasion the indefatigable Professor called at a farmhouse in the glen at eleven o'clock one night, seeking refreshment. "They brought him a bottle of whisky and a can of milk, which he mixed and consumed in two draughts from a huge bowl." No insignificant feat when one remembers the fiery, full-blooded liquor sold as whisky in some parts of the Highlands in pre-War days!

The hills now fell back, and the long, dreary, white glen reached away in front, bleak and silent. Here and there stood the ruined walls of the old clansmen's crofts, eloquent advertisement of the effect of a deer forest on the old order.

Always when passing through a glen where ruined cottages lie amongst the over-running bracken, there comes to my mind a verse from " Kenneth's Song." I cannot say it holds in this case, but many of the glens in our country are to-day stark and empty, only ruined walls where one time lived the happy clansmen, because the land was necessary for the deer.

> But the big-horned stag and his hinds, we know,
>   In the high corries ;
> And the salmon that swirls the pool below
>   Where the stream rushes,
> Are more than the hearts of men, and so
>   We leave thy green valley.

I was glad when the hills withdrew and the last mile or two changed to a tree-lined path, and so across an old bridge, past a ruined mill, and on to the main highway to Oban and the West, with Dalmally just a short walk ahead, and the crown of the road free of snow !

No part of this road could prove uninteresting for any man with eyes to see, as while now more open than in dark Glenorchy, every step reveals new and ever-changing views in a panorama of hill and glen.

Now we were almost at Dalmally, and from there my guide and travelling companion was taking the bus for somewhere on business of his own, but he accompanied me to the hotel for a moment or two as he was rather before his hour.

Here we met an old man who had lived all his years in a cottage on the hill-side, but his limited knowledge of English made conversation difficult. Indeed even his Gaelic was hard to follow, and it was only by slowly repeating his words that my ghillie friend and another native, sent for to help us to interpret, could with difficulty get his meaning.

When Pennant visited Dalmally many years ago, he made record of a family of smiths, MacNab by name, who had dwelt here, pursuing their avocation without a break in the direct family line since 1440.

There was no MacNab now, the old man said— the last of the line had died or left the place fully fifty years back. But he told us how one afternoon Duncan Ban M'Intyre, having killed a goat possessed of a wonderful horn, he detached it from the skull and brought it to MacNab the blacksmith, with a request that he should fit to it a blade and so make a sgain dhu.

MacNab was a wondrous craftsman, and he put all his skill and cunning into the work, so that the poet was delighted when the finished knife was handed to him.

" How much do I owe you, MacNab ? " queried the poet.

" Money could not buy its like," replied the blacksmith, " and for it money I shall not accept. Make a verse about it, and as masters we shall both be served."

And so Duncan Ban M'Intyre sang of it to the

eager smith, and it was this poem my old Highlander recited to us.

Then the bus arrived and my interpreter friends
bade me a hurried farewell—and so we were alone—
the old man, who was so anxious to tell me all he
knew—and I no less anxious to hear his experiences,
neither of us knowing what the other said ! I
wondered how the old-time travellers fared here
more than a century ago, but of course the Parish
Church minister was a ready friend, always glad to
meet wayfarers from the outer world.

An ancient divine who made a tour of this land
in 1803, has left a most interesting record of his
itinerary. He was accompanied by a " Mr S.," who
otherwise remains anonymous throughout.

Amongst other places, they visited Glenorchy,
coming by way of Loch Lomond-side, over the Rest
and by Inveraray and Cladich. A night was spent
at Luss, in hopes of seeing the Rev. Mr Stewart, held
in very high esteem by our author, for his translation
of the Scriptures into Gaelic, for which he received
the " inadequate recompense " of £500.

Mr Stewart was from home, but Mrs Stewart had
remained behind, and invited the tourists to partake
of breakfast. She treated the wanderers in a most
hospitable manner, and now may I quote :

" Leaving the lake, we turned towards Arroquar.
Here we stopped to recruit ourselves and our horse.
From this place I addressed the following letter to
Mrs Stuart :—

" ' MADAM,—As I never had the pleasure of
seeing you before, and perhaps never shall again, I
should be sorry to leave this part of the country

without expressing my sense of your kindness, and that of the other friends whom we parted with at Luss. If you are possessed of a diamond pencil I should be obliged to you if you would inscribe the following lines on one of the windows of the public house at your village:

> ' Whoe'er thou art that travell'st here like us,
> To view the wonders of romantic Luss,
> If mountains, woods, or lakes have charms for thee,
> Here all that's grand or beauteous shalt thou see,
> If manners sweet and kindness please thee more
> Than Lomond's heights, or lake, or wood-crown'd shore,
> Go, seek the manse, and in it thou shalt find,
> Whate'er is lovely in the human mind.' "

When Presbyterianism was established in this district Mr Dugald Lindsay, the Episcopalian minister, refused to conform to the new doctrine, and a probationer was sent to supersede him, but on arriving in his parish he found no house would receive him, and he had perforce to call upon Mr Lindsay for board and bed. That benign man made him welcome, well knowing that every hand was against the incomer.

On Sabbath morning old and young assembled in the churchyard long before the normal hour of worship, and when the new pastor arrived, accompanied by their faithful old minister, signs of annoyance and indignation were at once apparent.

But the murmurs were soon to give place to stronger action, and twelve men, fully armed, stepped forward, led by two pipers playing the march of death, and led the astonished Presbyterian to the boundary of the parish.

Q

There his captors made him swear never again to enter Glenorchy, and furthermore, not to lodge complaints for the acts committed against him that day. The oath was duly fulfilled, and Mr Lindsay remained to minister to his loyal parishioners undisturbed for fully thirty years.

The road was almost clear of snow when I left Dalmally.

A mile or two, and there, on a windswept hill, overlooking the scenes he loved and knew so well, stands the striking monument to Duncan Ban M'Intyre.

He was the Burns of the Gaelic-speaking race and sang to them in a way which stirred their hearts, yet, strange as it may seem, he could neither read nor write !

As a child, " Fair-haired Duncan of the Songs," as he became known to the dwellers in the glens, spent his early years on the hill-sides between Tyndrum and Glencoe.

Although a Jacobite at heart, the poet, because of his fealty to Breadalbane, fought against the Highlanders at the battle of Falkirk, and later, through the influence of his patron, he secured a position in the Edinburgh City Guard.

He died in Edinburgh in his eighty-ninth year, and was buried in the famous Greyfriars' Churchyard, but his heart was ever in his native glens—his fondest memories, of the hills and open spaces.

Duncan Ban M'Intyre was not alone in singing the charms of this rugged country-side.

Hammerton came here in 1852 and fell a victim to its graces. He dipped into its romantic legends and embalmed them in verse, illustrating the pages with his own pencil.

John Stuart Blackie, that modern knight-errant, knew every corrie, loved every stone, took them to his heart, and sang them in his warm, impulsive manner.

His great generous heart still beats amongst these western hills for those attuned to hear it. To read his lays by the fireside of a winter night when the far-off peaks are shrouded in mist, the glens choked with snow, and the wind screaming on the moors, is again to feel the spring of the heather beneath one's feet, to bring to life the sleeping pageant of its beauty.

Over there rises Cruachan, alone with its Arctic-clad companions. Below lies Loch Awe—to-day cold and glassy—no sun glinting on its blue waves.

Loch Awe is the centre-piece, the intimate heart of one of the most exquisite sections of Scottish beauty, crowned with the romance of deeds long past, a land too beautiful to paint with pen or palette.

Above, towers Cruachan—from which is derived the slogan of the Campbells—guarding the Pass, with a scarf of cloud trailing from his head. A noble ben, some twenty miles round the base, but looking more massive and imposing a few miles off.

How these great immutable hills sprang into existence I cannot say—some mighty cataclysm when the world was young; but I can give you the true origin of Loch Awe, where once was a smiling, fertile glen.

Here it is—ascribed to Ossian.

" Bera the Aged dwelt in a cave in the rock. She

was the daughter of a sage. Long was the line of her fathers—and she was the last of her race. Large and fertile were her possessions, hers the beautiful vales below; hers the cattle which roamed on the hills around.

" To her was left a heritage that she must every night, ere sunset, place a certain stone over a spring on the hill-side. One day, wearied with the chase, she sat down to rest beneath a tree. The sun was strong—and she slept. She slept until morning, and when she arose to go and remove the stone, the spring had burst from its bounds and her inheritance was under water. So was created Loch Awe."

Bera appears to have been a wholly disagreeable person, and no good neighbour for the more industrious section of the folks hereabouts. She dwelt somewhere in the most inaccessible part of the mountains, and, it is claimed, could step from one district to another with consummate ease. When the inhabitants did anything to offend her she sent great floods to spoil their crops and generally kept the district in a ferment.

An ancient philosopher, who inquired into these charges brought against Bera the Aged, exonerated her completely and laid the responsibility on nothing more romantic than water-spouts. Personally, I have an unreasoning antipathy against philosophers and cold-blooded logicians of this sort, and unreservedly acclaim Bera as the true cause of all the mischief.

The island of Fraoch Eilan has its modern romance, but here is one of its old-time legends.

Once in the long ago Fraoch island was an enchanted garden guarded by a dragon, whose duty it was to keep inviolate the luscious golden fruit which flourished there.

There was a gallant warrior named Fraoch, and his beautiful sweetheart, Mego, was, woman-like, consumed by longing for the forbidden fruit. Fraoch, like the fearless heart he was, swam to the island to battle with its guardian if need be, but possess some of the fruit he must.

The dragon saw his approach, and a fearful battle ensued, in which both were slain. Mego the Fair died shortly afterwards of a broken heart.

There is no more strikingly situated fastness of other days in all broad Scotland than Kilchurn Castle. Picturesque to a degree, romance and legend seem in fancy to cling to its broken walls like a mantle of the past.

At one time Kilchurn occupied an island, but the Orchy has been quietly at work for generations silting up the loch.

But that does not matter now. No longer are its stout walls called upon to defend the Campbell owners ; never again will axe and spear and claymore flash in the torchlight, or the great ben give back the shouts of struggling warriors. To-day all is peace.

As recently as the '45, Kilchurn was garrisoned by royal troops, but now decay and neglect have played their part well, and only the shell remains, hoary with time and steeped in untold memories.

The very building of the castle is of itself a tale of romance. Sir Colin Campbell of Glenorchy was a Crusader. Ere bidding farewell to his young wife he cut his ring into two parts, one of which he handed to his lady, telling her that if he fell in the wars he would cause his half of the ring to be sent home, but while he was alive, it would never leave his person.

Years passed and there came no word from the Holy Land.

All this time Sir Colin was taking part in many a stricken field, but oftentimes his heart would be in green Glenorchy, and then he would send his lady a message of good cheer by one of his trusty followers. But none of these couriers ever reached his mistress on far Lochawe-side.

Many suitors made advances to the waiting lady, the most persistent of all being Baron Neil Mac-Corquodale, whose lands marched with those of Sir Colin. He it was who had intercepted the returning couriers and slain them so that their good news should not be delivered. And then he bethought him of a still blacker villainy; nothing less than prevailing on a friend in the Holy Land to send home a message that Sir Colin was indeed dead.

Even then the lady hesitated, but at last she gave a halting promise that when the castle was finished, she would wed her neighbour.

Slowly the time passed, but at last the fortress was completed, and, pressed by MacCorquodale, she gave a reluctant consent, and the nuptial arrangements were put in hand.

Meanwhile Sir Colin, as the result of a dream, decided to return to his native land.

On the wedding morn the usual motley crowd was gathered around the castle door, amongst them one man of outstanding person, bearded and bronzed by the sun, who demanded a cup of wine from the hands of the bride. Quaffing it to the dregs, the stranger dropped something into the drinking-cup and handed it back to her with the remark that it was now more valuable than before.

A quick glance disclosed the half ring, and with a glad cry she threw herself into Sir Colin's arms.

The loyal clansmen acclaimed their chief, and as a token of joy and goodwill, MacCorquodale was allowed to depart uninjured and forgiven.

Later, on the death of Sir Colin, his son, Sir Colin Dubh, revenged himself on MacCorquodale, and in just retribution took possession of his lands.

To-day, only some wheeling gulls scream round the decaying towers, and night finds no beacon from its fallen ports.

This must have been a solitary if peaceful spot, when one summer evening in 1755 Campbell of Inverawe was quietly enjoying its beauty. Whatever his thoughts, they were rudely broken by a man, nearly spent, who came running across a shoulder of the great ben and appealed for sanctuary. He had slain a man in anger, and his enemies were hot on his trail.

Inverawe pledged his word to protect him from the avengers, and knowing every rock and crevice on Cruachan-side, he guided the outcast to a lonely cave, and promised to return with food when the pursuers had gone.

On his way down the mountain-side he met one of his clansmen, who explained that he was searching for a murderer who had mysteriously disappeared. The searcher added that the man whose life had been taken was no other than Inverawe's foster-brother, to whom he was particularly attached.

During the night the spirit of his foster-brother appeared to Campbell and demanded blood for blood. A second night the vision appeared demanding vengeance on his murderer, and so wrought on Campbell's mind that next morning he went to the cave and ordered the guilty man to make good his escape.

That evening the ghost again appeared at Inverawe's bedside, bitterly complained at the failure to avenge his wrongs, and ere departing warned his foster-brother that they would meet at Ticonderoga. In the morning Campbell went to the cave determined to avenge his brother and bring peace to his own mind, but the murderer had fled.

The whole circumstance so preyed on Campbell that it was with a feeling of relief he received orders —he was a major in the 42nd Regiment—to proceed overseas.

Do what he would the ghostly threat of Ticonderoga haunted him, until at last he unburdened his mind to his fellow-officers.

In due course the regiment was ordered to advance upon St Louis, when one of the officers discovered that the Indian name for the place was Ticonderoga. The town was stormed, but amongst those who fell, mortally wounded, was Campbell of Inverawe, whose dying words were that the place was not called St Louis, but Ticonderoga, for he had seen his brother !

R. L. Stevenson has made the tale his own and retold it in verse.

It was here, on the side of Cruachan, that Bruce, nobly assisted by his great captain, Douglas, fully revenged himself on M'Dougall of Lorne.

A desperate battle took place amongst the rocks on the steep hill-side, and ultimately the M'Dougalls' defence was broken and they fled before the royal forces. Many were hunted down amongst the rocks and slain, others were drowned in the loch below, and John of Lorne, Chief of the M'Dougalls, only escaped by means of a boat.

The King had now the upper hand in the Westlands, and as a result of this fierce battle he deprived Lorne of a great part of his lands.

The day was drawing late now, and I was thankful for a " lift " from a friendly chauffeur, and soon we were covering the hill miles to Inveraray at a fine pace.

Down through the tree-lined road, wintry looking to-day, where only yesterday, it seemed, the wild flowers and moss had made the way gay for the passer, and then the glint of the loch as we passed through the archway into the town.

XVIII

FROM MY WINDOW AGAIN

The melancholy days are come,
The saddest of the year,
Of wailing winds, and naked woods,
And meadows brown and sere.

W. CULLEN BRYANT

ALL too soon the pageant of the seasons passes. Spring with her adolescence and promise, Summer and her fulfilment, Autumn with her ripe experience, gradually merge and give place to the snows and desolation of winter.

To-day the burnished browns and russets, crimsons and gold are rapidly disappearing before the windy buffetings, and already the bare skeletons of once leafy woods are waving gaunt arms above the withered bracken. Every fresh gust produces its macabre dance of fluttering leaves, and the moss is happed beneath a rustling brown coverlet.

Time to draw the curtains again and turn of an evening to the book-shelves, rovering days behind us for a spell. The hill-sides and drove roads are closed for a season—not from choice but of necessity.

Where only a week or two ago the mountain burn fell down the slopes in a splashing cascade, to-day a torrent rages. Placid brown streams of yesterday have suddenly changed their character, and are rushing through the glens, churned, tormented, and unfordable.

Heather braes are now watery moss-hags, dangerous in places, and every trace of past glories has been lost in the blackened or bleached wastes.

On the lowland fields may be seen vast congregations of stalking rooks, strangely silent and preoccupied. Occasional bands of peesweeps on the marshy places seem lost in contemplation of the changing scene.

One friend has gone completely from my ken in the old tortoise, now snug amongst some hay in the potting-shed, but, as always in this world, another has taken his place. The pert robin has turned up again to haunt the garden and collect his tribute until the dark days pass, as self-contained and sure of his welcome as if he had never basely deserted me in the springtime without a farewell chirp, although well I know he will show the same spirit whenever the bright days return and joy o' living entices him once more to his country seat, his social habits being for all the world like those of some prosperous city magnate.

By now the bens have donned their white nightcaps and, tucked beneath their blankets of mist and cloud, will sleep dormant and undisturbed for long, ere adventurous feet bring them back for a period to the living world.

Slush and mud in the city streets, but out there in the silent glens the moon looks down on the white-clad spaces, and the old drove road winds deserted and alone save perhaps when the hill-fox brings home a mountain hare as proof of good hunting or the stags come down in search of better feeding.

The trusty stout shoes are greased and stored away against more likely times. The old ash plant must needs rest content until the burns sing again and the enveloping mists yield to a warmer sun.

> Boughs are daily rifled,
> By the gusty thieves,
> And the Book of Nature
> Getteth short of leaves.

Yesterday morning the field which fronts my home was heavily populated with gulls, and that old-time wisdom and experience which is safely chronicled in our proverbs, told me bad weather was in store.

> Seagull, seagull, sit on the sand,
> It's never guid weather when you're on the land.

True it proved, and by night rain was blattering on the office window and the wind, blowing strongly from the west across the well-loved hills, was making an eerie wailing amongst the chimney-cans.

Pausing from my task for a moment I glanced at the wet, deserted street. A taxi splashed past on its way to theatre or station, and a solitary policeman, mushroom-like under his short glistening cape, was slowly pacing along, head down against the blast.

No night this to be abroad. Better to work an hour longer and hope the weather might abate.

Back to the task in hand then—but somehow the momentary break had cut athwart my thoughts and concentration came slowly.

Only for the wind and blatter of rain the outside world appeared strangely silent. Rain drives the street people under cover quickly of an evening.

And then suddenly there came a loud, high-pitched cry—"hioch, hioch" it sounded, and brought me from my desk to the window again.

Below was a drove of cattle, obviously being driven from Merklands Wharf to the market in High Street, and the men in charge were shouting and occasionally thwacking the laggards in their anxiety to get the job done and be free to shelter from the drenching rain.

Steam was rising in a cloud from the great untidy-looking herd, and occasionally a panic-stricken, or maybe only more enterprising beast, would break from the drove and, inspired by what whim I know not, make a bolt for a side street.

Then would follow a wild race between man and beast, and the great lumbering, wild-eyed brute would be driven back at the run to join his fellows.

Two or three enthusiastic urchins, unpaid but willing workers, ran alongside and helped to guard the passes, and added to the general confusion and hubbub.

And then the houses and cobbled streets fell away from my city eyes, and of a sudden I looked back into the past.

Some one, I think John Buchan, says the old drover race is dead and their place shall know them no more, but I always *sensed* that this was wrong.

Now I know that when all is quiet on the hill-side and in the strath, when the motors have deserted the highways for a space, and the men of affairs, having slaughtered their grouse and fished for their salmon, have gone back to office and bar, the old reivers lurk behind the scattered rocks, wild-eyed cattle are driven at the run, and the road collop is bestowed as toll of clan rights and privileges.

There before my eyes, the rain-dashed window, the street lamps and high buildings, faded into mist and gave place to the dark hill-side where away in front, faintly marked amongst the over-growing heather and bracken, wound the old-time drove road.

Above, the scudding clouds and a silver-horned moon giving a weird, diffused light. Of stars there were none, and the distant peaks stood black as ebony amidst the silence.

One or two isolated trees were bent towards the east, sure sign of prevailing winds from the Hebridean seas, and a fox barked somewhere in the distance.

And then along the twisting path came a great herd of shaggy cattle! Here and there one paused to nose the runnel of water which died in the heather a yard farther on, but always a guttural shout from behind kept them steadily on the move.

If the kyloe were shaggy and rough and unkempt, how can I describe their owners? Bearded, garbed in mud-stained tartans, armed with claymore and pistol, they looked fit wardens for their charges. Strong and active, inured to hill and weather, ruddy and fearless, they were making for the cattle tryst, and had been some days on the journey. Rain and wind meant nothing to them, and they would sleep, fireless, by their herd.

The moon was glinting on the loch now, and the band was making for water ere rounding up for the night, to be off again with the call of the grouse in the dim morning light.

A hard life—but a man's life—and as I stood from my vantage and watched them pass, envious of their freedom, a beast broke from the herd, and the running drover, with his shout and the thwack of the stick, shattered the spell, and the streets crowded back again to my vision as the drove road faded out.

There in the glistening, rain-swept causeys the cattle were disappearing, the steam cloud rising white above them in the glare of the overhead arc-lamps, and with a distant-shouted "hioch" they were gone.

Never again would they graze in the fresh green pastures or rest by the burn-side when the sun was high : but for me, I knew that over there behind the slates and chimney cans, far beyond the shining lamps and car rails, lay the hills and glens with their glamour and their urge : that some day again I would see in their beauty the early primrose and the flaming gorse—the dog-roses and the purple blanket of heather : that the open road would call me when the bondage of winter was over and past, call with an insistence that I could not resist. Who that knows it can forget the heartening smell of a wood fire ; the corn bowing to the whispering breeze, white clouds against a blue sky, and the glory of the rowans in their pride ?   Above the croon of the burn would come the trill of a lark—and alluring and beckoning, elusive and compelling, the winding lochside road !

A stronger gust of wind, a blash of rain on the office window, and as I turned to complete my work it was to leave a vision of deserted street, with the yellow lamp-light casting dismal shadows over all.

The solitary policeman with his glistening mushroom cape at the corner, dreaming perhaps of the sheiling and surf-tormented rocks of his boyhood, was alone on his city beat.